Short Stories

For teen girls

12 FEEL-GOOD AND INSPIRATIONAL TALES

Who Are We?

"La Bibli des Ados" is a collection of funny, original and sometimes offbeat books strictly for teens!

If you like these kind of books, you will love all the others already released and those to come ;)

You can access our store by scanning the QR code below directly with your smartphone's camera:

ISBN: 9798315020400
First Edition – March 2025

2025 © La Bibli des Ados - All rights reserved

"Any full or partial representation or reproduction without the consent of the author or their rights holders is unlawful. This applies equally to translation, adaptation, transformation, arrangement, or reproduction by any means or process."

Table of Contents

The Value of Money — 7

Eco-Anxiety — 17

Beating Shyness with Talent! — 27

The Rules of Love — 41

The First Time... — 49

Matthew the Liar — 61

As Ugly as a Toad — 71

Anorexia — 83

Finding Your Path — 93

Courtney. Sixteen. A Short Fuse — 105

The Bully — 117

A Filter Between You and Yourself — 129

The Value of Money

The Value of Money

For the past few months, home has been a war zone. Not the kind with shouting or broken dishes, but a constant, suffocating tension, like standing on the edge of an explosion that never quite happens. In history class, the teacher talked about the Cold War between the U.S. and the USSR. Yeah, that's exactly it, a Cold War at home! And in the middle of senior year, no less. Perfect.

Lina is furious. Her mom refuses everything, all the time, with the same excuse: You don't know the value of money. The most infuriating thing about adults? Their habit of repeating the same tired phrases, refusing to negotiate, clinging to their so-called principles. Worst of all, they don't get it—life as a high schooler today is nothing like what they knew. Maybe they got by with just a handful of outfits all year, oblivious to fashion, to what people thought of them. Maybe they never went out. Or maybe they've just forgotten what it's like, how you don't fit in unless you play the game.

At eighteen, you're not really a kid anymore. Still, Lina wasn't about to explain to her mom that guys notice curves and that her clothes were supposed to make her look good. She also wasn't going to admit that, during free periods—when a teacher was out—she hung out at the little café by the gas station instead of sitting in study hall. Getting treated once or twice was fine, but lately, she was starting to look like a real freeloader.

"But Mom, it's not like I'm asking for a paycheck! Just enough to go shopping with Juliette on Saturday!"

— *The Value of Money* —

"You're driving me crazy, Lina. Seriously, you are! Don't you have anything better to do than waste time in overpriced stores?!"

Her mom isn't exactly rich, that much is true. She's raising Lina on her own and doing everything she can to make sure she never goes without. She works as a nursing assistant, not exactly making a fortune, and until now, Lina had always been proud of her. Proud of this woman who pours all her energy, all her warmth, into the kids at the pediatric ward. But frustration builds up, and the more it does, the more Lina finds herself seeing her mother in a different light. And she hates it.

"I was young once too, you know. I wanted to show off, impress boys. But trust me, that's not the way to earn respect."

Oh, here we go. A confession! So she does understand. She's been there! And yet, she's still lecturing her. What a nightmare. And of course, she keeps going.

"And anyway, if you want to buy yourself some clothes, you just need to get a job!"

"Oh yeah? Doing what?"

"The hospital is looking for extra cleaning staff over the break."

"Cleaning staff?!"

"Yeah, you'd be taking care of patient rooms and common areas—like, the hallways.

"And… does it pay well?"

"No, but it does pay. It's a tough job, but rewarding. Hygiene is essential for welcoming and caring for patients."

"I'm in!"

"You sure? Want me to talk to my supervisor about it tomorrow?"

"I said I'm in!"

It's the best evening in a long time. Lina sets the table without being asked, clears the dishes with a smile, even suggests watching a movie with her mom. A new chapter is beginning! The pay wouldn't be huge, and for now, it was only two weeks of work over the break. But with free meals and a place to stay, she didn't have many expenses. Everything would go straight into her pocket. Or more accurately, into the pockets of that mid-season jacket she spotted last week.

On the first Monday of break, she feels pure excitement.. This is real life, the kind where you rely only on yourself. Finally, real responsibilities! Sure, it wouldn't last long, but it is just enough to prove herself and maybe land a hospital job this summer, something to build real savings.

When her mother introduces her to the team in the nurses'

—— The Value of Money ——

lounge of the Internal Medicine ward, Lina suddenly feels a little less at ease. This is the adult world—exactly what she wanted—but not many people share her enthusiasm. They welcome her, they smile, but she can still sense the exhaustion. Maybe even some tension. She'll be spending the day with Madison, a woman in her thirties with messy hair who seems to take her role as a trainer very seriously.

"As long as you do your job properly, you won't have any problems here. But you're not the first teenager to start, and we've seen how it goes. After a few days, things often start getting sloppy. If you start 'forgetting' rooms, ignoring patients, or stretching out your breaks, I won't be able to help you."

Alright. Crystal clear. Lina had no intention of slacking off— quite the opposite—but that warning left a bad taste in her mouth. If this was going to feel like being monitored at school, no thanks. *Madison seems nice enough,* she thought, *but she'd better not talk to me like a little kid all the time...*

The Internal Medicine ward houses a wide range of patients. In the first room she enters, pushing her small cleaning cart, Lina finds a man in his fifties. He looks miserable, his eyes fixed on the TV mounted on the wall. Just before stepping in, Madison leans toward her and murmurs that he just arrived. She overheard his wife talking to the doctor in a worried tone. He's been losing weight for weeks and running recurring fevers. They've brought him here to run tests and figure out what's going on. t's not exactly part of the cleaning job, but Madison explains that with patients like him, it's important to

— The Value of Money —

be friendly, even chat a little if he seems like he needs it.

"You'll quickly realize that cleaning is only part of the job. There's also a social side to it. You're young, you're healthy, and you're full of energy—you have the power to brighten their day. And that matters. You don't have to, but trust me, you'll feel more useful and more fulfilled if you go along with it."

Of course, Lina agrees, but that doesn't mean she feels confident. It's a real responsibility. Still, if she's going to go along with it, she might as well dive right in…

"Good morning, Mr. Reynolds! How are you today?"

"Good morning, miss."

"So, what are you watching?"

"I'd like to listen to my show, if you don't mind…"

Well, that failed. The guy had basically just told her to shut up. Without saying a word, Lina gets to work, following her supervisor's instructions. She doesn't let it show, but it stings. How are you supposed to help people who don't even want to talk to you? She won't be trying to start any more conversations today. Madison, who clearly picks up on the awkwardness, doesn't say a thing. She just leads Lina to the next room as if nothing happened. For now, it's all about learning: how to tell the different cleaning products apart, how to use the mop without wearing herself out, and most importantly, understanding why this job matters.

— *The Value of Money* —

"Lina, do you know what a nosocomial infection is?"

"A what?"

"A nosocomial infection. It's an infection you catch while staying in the hospital. You come in for one thing and end up with something else. The longer a patient stays, the higher the risk. It's just statistics."

"Sh— I mean... Sorry... But that's horrible!"

"Yep. And that's exactly why your job matters, to reduce that risk. In most cases, infections spread through hands. See that light switch? Looks harmless, right? But all it takes is one visitor touching it without washing their hands first, leaving behind a germ that some of our patients' immune systems just can't fight off."

"So... I could actually kill someone? If I don't clean properly, I could put patients in danger?"

"Exactly. Now do you see why your job is so important?"

The week drags on. Despite her efforts, despite all the cheerfulness she tries to bring to her interactions, Lina is met with nothing but indifference. Some patients hide it better than others, but it's always there. Most of them respond half-heartedly, making it clear they don't take her seriously.

Her body aches. She's exhausted, physically and mentally. Was it really worth it? Money isn't easy to earn, but there's no

— *The Value of Money* —

way she's admitting that when her mom questions her every night.

"So, how was your day?" her mother asks.

"It was fine."

"What does fine even mean? That doesn't tell me anything! Do you get along with your coworkers? I hear you're pretty quiet. Madison says you do what's expected of you, but you don't exactly look happy…"

"Oh great, so you're spying on me now?"

"No, I'm just checking in, that's all. Don't start."

"I told you I'm fine, that's it. I spend my day mopping floors and scrubbing door handles… It's not exactly living the dream. What do you want me to say?"

"If you want to quit, just say so."

"I don't want to quit, Mom, please. I'm just tired. Can you understand that?"

But on the last Saturday of her so-called "break," wandering through the mall with Juliette, Lina does her best to put on a good face.

"It's actually pretty interesting, even if it's not easy. Some people there are really struggling. Super lonely, you know? I feel like it helps them when someone just takes the time to talk."

Juliette, however, quickly loses interest, her attention drifting to the store windows.

"Oh my God, look at this shirt! I love the color. Apparently, they're having a sale. Let's check it out?"

"If you want."

A little stung, Lina follows, dragging her feet. Around her, the world feels both familiar and strangely distant. The same stores, the same displays—everything looks as it always has, yet suddenly, something feels missing. She can't look at anything without noticing the price. Things have value. A value they didn't seem to have before. Or rather, it's money that suddenly holds value in Lina's eyes.

A little unsettled and not wanting her lack of enthusiasm to show, Lina pretends to browse through each aisle, but she can't shake the thought of prices. How many clothes could she actually afford with her vacation paycheck? Not many, apparently... Juliette suddenly steps in front of her, a triumphant look on her face, holding out a corduroy overshirt.

"This is perfect for you, look! Are you gonna try it on?"

Awkward. Juliette's parents weren't exactly rich, but they were well-off. Every week, they gave her pocket money—something Lina had always felt a little jealous of. Then again, she had always suspected their generosity had more to do with making up for their absence. A way to compensate for how little time they actually spent at home, caught up in their demanding jobs.

Most of the time, to save face and hide how little money she actually had, Lina played the role of the picky shopper, the one who never found anything to her taste. That way, she could still enjoy the thrill of trying on clothes—free of charge—while imagining a massive wardrobe stretching across an entire wall of her bedroom. But today, she didn't have the heart to pretend.

"Oh no, forget it."

"What? But it's gorgeous! It would look amazing on you, just try it!"

"I don't feel like it."

Juliette, caught off guard by her cold tone, quietly puts the shirt back on the rack and walks out of the store without another word. Lina follows.

"Sorry, I don't know what got into me."

"It's fine. I'm heading home, it's getting dark."

How was she supposed to tell Juliette, plainly, that she couldn't afford everything she wanted? Before, she would have been embarrassed—ashamed, even—of coming from a

—— The Value of Money ——

modest background. But today, it felt different. She hadn't kept quiet out of shame, but to avoid making Juliette uncomfortable. Her friend had never had to think about money, never had to measure its worth. Pointing it out to her now would only feel awkward and unfair.

Back home, Lina finds her mother rearranging the living room.

"I was thinking of moving the couch against the wall. Can you help me?"

"Coming, Mom!"

After what feels like a hundred adjustments—shifting the couch three times, moving the small bookshelf, swapping out the desk and living room lamps, sorting through knickknacks—Lina hears her mother, out of breath, say:

"By the way! Did you find that jacket?"

"No, I think I'll just stick with the one I have."

"That's a shame. You haven't stopped talking about it."

"Sounds like you don't know the value of money, Mom!"

And with that, she hands her a small, neatly wrapped gift. She had also come to understand the value of her mother.

Eco-Anxiety

Eco-Anxiety

It all started during geography class. Mr. Carter was captivating—the kind of teacher you only meet once or twice in your school years. He was close to retirement, yet his passion for teaching remained intact. Every lesson brought a new discovery. And not always an academic one. He loved talking to us about current events, daily life, and the way he saw society and the world of tomorrow. Unlike other teachers, he didn't spend his time lecturing us. I never once heard him compare us to previous generations. Never once did he put us down. Despite his age, he understood teenagers. He knew that being an adolescent wasn't easy, that we were torn between childhood and the adulthood rushing toward us. He had faith in us. He trusted us.

One Monday morning, while the class was still struggling to shake off the weekend, he suddenly paused mid-sentence and turned to look out the window. We're lucky—our school is surrounded by greenery, and from his classroom, you can see tree branches almost brushing against the glass.

"I spent Sunday in the countryside with my grandson. Victor is seven. You should have seen him running through the grass, he was so happy. Then we took a walk in the woods. Such a peaceful moment..."

I felt the whole class sit up, as if we were one single student. Whenever Mr. Carter started sharing personal stories, it was never just small talk. It always led to something. Where was he taking us this time? And besides, it was also a sign that we were about to drift away from the lesson—which was never bad news. In moments like these, we could close our history and geography textbooks. We also knew there probably wouldn't be anything to write down in our notebooks. Another win.

Still, there was something off about him. He looked... a little sad. I could sense that something was different.

"Will you be able to do the same?" he asked. "I mean, when you're my age, will you still be able to take your grandchildren for a walk in the woods? Will there even be any woods left...?"

Jeanne spoke up. She was kind of the class know-it-all, but I had to admit—she was usually spot on. We all secretly envied the special connection she had with Mr. Carter. They understood each other.

"Sir, could it be that you're suffering from eco-anxiety?"

"Here we go, she's making up words again!" Lucas chimed in, but mostly just to get a laugh.

Mr. Carter looked at both of them with kindness. He stayed quiet for a moment before finally replying.

"It is indeed a fairly recent and not very commonly used term. But eco-anxiety refers to a real phenomenon. It is a deep concern about the future of our planet. I've often talked in class about the impacts of climate change—purely in a theoretical way, as part of the lesson. But yesterday, I felt that anxiety like never before. I'm sorry to lay this on you, but I feel incredibly sad."

Eco-anxiety. Some words just stick with you. At that moment, I found it interesting, but I didn't think much more about it. Especially since our poor teacher quickly pulled himself together and, for once, sent us back to the textbook. Story time was over.

That evening, on my way home, the moment replayed in my mind. Eco-anxiety. Wasn't that, in the end, a completely normal reaction? I heard about environmental issues all the time—on TV, on social media—but I had never really paid much attention. I'd seen terrifying videos about the consequences of climate change, but let's be honest—TikTok's endless scroll wasn't exactly the best place for deep reflection.

At dinner, while a mind-numbingly boring news segment droned on in the background, I decided to ask my parents.

"We talked about eco-anxiety at school today. Mr. Carter was really upset. He told us the world is changing so fast that nature might completely disappear one day."

My dad ran a hand over his face. His signature gesture of irritation. He did it at least ten times a day. As if life was just a series of annoyances and frustrations. I love him, but he can't stand anything. Especially not new ideas. To him, they're just trends, nonsense, marketing ploys. Nothing is ever genuine in his eyes. Everything is manipulation.

"Oh great, just what we needed! Do you really think we don't have bigger problems? Have you seen the unemployment rate? Do you have any idea how much I have to pay in taxes this year? Don't start with all these new teenage obsessions. You all live such cushy lives that you have to invent anxieties! It's insane. Let's see if you still have time for your so-called eco-anxiety once you have a job."

My mother cut him off.

"She just said a word. You're getting worked up over nothing. Sweetheart, what did you talk about in class? Are you actually worried? Tell me."

"No, it's just... there's a huge problem, and if we don't do anything, the future is going to be a disaster. But Dad doesn't care! I'm the one who's going to have to live on a ruined planet. My kids will too. You've spent your whole life consuming without a second thought, and now you can't even consider changing your habits to save people and biodiversity!"

My dad was starting to lose his temper.

"Oh, right. So you're going to save the whales and the seals with your little geography lessons? Tell you what—start by giving up your smartphone. And next time you're at McDonald's with your friends, don't forget to order a burger without the meat. Don't be like me—be responsible, my dear."

— *Eco-Anxiety* —

Impossible to have a real conversation. Anyway, it was clear to me now—aside from people like Mr. Carter, eco-anxiety was something only young people felt. And that made sense. It was our world to fix.

That argument with my dad made me realize something: my responsibility. My duty to future generations. Most people probably thought like him, no doubt about it. And that selfishness would be our downfall. I'd bring it up with Mr. Carter on Thursday. Something had to be done.

He met with me at the end of class. As the last students trickled out, glancing at me with curiosity, I ran through my arguments in my head. I was lucky to have such a great teacher—someone who could even become an ally, maybe even a partner in this. Exactly what I needed.

Mr. Carter remained just as he always was—open, welcoming, and kind. He gestured for me to sit and asked me to explain what had brought me to him.

"You were right, sir. Deforestation is accelerating at an alarming rate! More and more species are disappearing—we're living through the sixth mass extinction."

"Yes, my dear… It's heartbreaking."

"We have to do something. Everyone needs to know."

"If I understand correctly, you'd like to do a presentation on the topic. That's an excellent idea, I must say. I commend you—it will be very valuable for your classmates. We can already start thinking about an angle. You could focus on the depletion of natural resources or extreme weather events—those are concrete examples that resonate with most people."

"You don't understand. I'm not asking for an assignment, and I don't want to give a lecture! I want to act, sir! Act before it's too late!"

"And what exactly do you have in mind?"

"A bold action at school. We could sabotage the plumbing so that everyone realizes what it's like to live without water. Repairs would probably take a few hours, maybe a day, but it would be a powerful way to raise awareness. What do you think?"

"Claire… While I deeply respect your commitment, I have to warn you—actions like that could get you into serious trouble."

"I don't care! You don't seem to understand—I'm talking about survival on Earth, and you're worried about my school record!"

"Activism doesn't have to be destructive, you know. That's often how we recognize the early signs of extremist movements… or even terrorism. Remember our lesson on—"

"I'm really disappointed, Mr. Carter. You've always

—— Eco-Anxiety ——

encouraged us to stand by our values and fight for the future. I'm quoting you on that."

Realizing just how wrong I had been, I decided to leave the room. If Mr. Carter held it against me, so be it. But who should really feel ashamed? The student who walks out without saying goodbye, or the teacher who betrays his own convictions? There was nothing to expect from the older generations. They were incapable of thinking beyond their own lives, of seeing the future as something they had a role in shaping. The world of tomorrow belonged to those who chose to build it today. And I had no intention of being intimidated by the threat of a disciplinary hearing or a report. Sure, Mr. Carter had been gentle, but at the end of the day, how was his passive cowardice any different from my father's blunt indifference?

Even though I had initially wanted to handle this on my own, I needed to involve Savannah and Malik, my two friends. Two people who actually cared about the environment. Savannah's parents were active in a climate action group. Malik was the class scientist—the kind of person who loved numbers and facts, but who, I suspected, was also itching for a cause worth fighting for. Maybe this would be his chance to start a revolution alongside me. Data and statistics meant nothing compared to real experience. By cutting off the school's water supply, we would force everyone to confront their own dependence—and their responsibility. If you need water, then protect it!

My two accomplices, however, reacted just like Mr. Carter.

The same hesitation, the same cautious excuses. "Think about the consequences." "What about your future?" "Your dad is going to lose it." A nightmare. I couldn't understand how people could be so cowardly—so obsessed with what others might think. To me, it felt like a personal insult. A betrayal. And I made sure they knew it.

The days that followed were silent. Completely. Not a word. To anyone. If the whole world was going to run from its responsibilities, then I would run from the whole world. A personal strike. Now convinced that the worst was inevitable, I couldn't see the future with even the slightest trace of hope. Sinking deeper into despair, I found myself utterly alone. To everyone else, I was the weirdo. The wild girl. The one who talked to trees. I lost my friends, and things with my parents became strained.

Mr. Carter watched my withdrawal in silence, choosing not to interfere. And for that, I was grateful. Since our argument over my sabotage plan, we hadn't spoken a single word to each other. Then, one Monday morning, as the class struggled to summon the energy to face the start of the week, he set down his marker and walked over to the window, a blissful smile spreading across his face.

"Victor, my grandson, turned eight yesterday. We celebrated his birthday as a family. What a joy it was to be together. After lunch, we took a walk in the woods, and I realized something. Nature is beautiful when it's shared. You need at least two people to say, 'Look, isn't it beautiful?'. It's in the care we show for one another today that we'll find the strength and

Eco-Anxiety

wisdom to solve the problems of tomorrow."

Seventy-five percent of species are destined to disappear in the coming centuries. Okay. But I couldn't carry the weight of the world on my shoulders alone. I will take this journey toward nature. But it will be with others and with joy.

Beating Shyness with Talent!

― *Beating Shyness with Talent!* ―

Miles had always been a quiet, observant boy, finding joy in the small, simple moments of life in his little town. He had two friends—two boys just as shy as he was, not very popular, but fascinating. The three of them arrived at school together and left side by side. Inseparable throughout the day, they sat through their classes without much interest, eagerly waiting for recess, when they could indulge in their favorite activity: coming up with "projects."

Their parents, teasingly calling them the *Musketeers*, often joked about their shared passion for science. Not school science—not math or biology the way it was taught in class—but rather the wild, futuristic possibilities of technology. They were convinced that the future would be incredible, and more than anything, they wanted to be part of it.

"Can you imagine when we have bionic arms?"

"Totally! Two insanely strong arms that let you lift *anything*!"

"Yeah, they should make special ones for firefighters. Picture this: a highway accident, one of the passengers is thrown through the windshield and ends up trapped under the car. The specialized firefighter arrives, his bionic arm wired to his skeleton and nervous system, and just lifts the wreck effortlessly."

"That would be awesome! And it could create jobs for people with disabilities. If someone's missing a limb, they could just get a mechanical prosthetic and be super useful in jobs that require strength…"

—— *Beating Shyness with Talent!* ——

These kinds of discussions lasted the entire lunch break. At two o'clock, they'd split up, each heading to their own class. Then they'd pick up right where they left off at three, and later, after school, continuing their exchange in Miles's backyard.

Most of their classmates saw them as geeky weirdos, but they didn't care. They had found each other, and that was enough. But the truth was a little more complicated. All three boys struggled with the same shyness. Social interactions never came easy to them. In a way, they had simply combined their individual loneliness and turned it into something that made them happy. A simple, quiet happiness—one that was suddenly shattered.

Miles's mother had just been transferred for work. They had to move immediately, and he would be starting at a new school. The news hit like a shockwave. It was so abrupt that the three of them couldn't even bring themselves to say goodbye. It was too painful, and deep down, each of them clung to the hope that maybe, somehow, it wouldn't actually happen. Their parents, noticing the situation, promised to arrange regular meetups. But in cases like this, promises were just words meant to make everyone feel better. Reality had a way of taking over, pushing even the best intentions aside.

A new school, new challenges—Miles had no choice but to adapt.

Miles's first day at Jefferson Middle School was even harder than he had imagined. The whispers started the moment he

—— Beating Shyness with Talent! ——

stepped into his new eighth-grade class. Sitting in the last row, he tried to make himself invisible, but his plain clothes and messy hair seemed to make him stand out even more. Over and over, he caught snippets of hushed conversations—"the new kid"—always buried within sentences he couldn't fully decipher. People were talking about him. A lot. And even if he couldn't make out exactly what they were saying, he could feel it. There wasn't much kindness in the air. There were the muffled laughs, the stares that lingered a second too long before quickly looking away. And worst of all—the teachers, who thought they were helping by calling on him constantly.

"So, Miles, are you settling in?"

"Where did you leave off in English at your old school?"

"Why don't we let Miles share his thoughts?"

Pure horror. Absolute humiliation. Blending in was impossible. And the worst was yet to come.

For three weeks now, Miles had been waiting it out, keeping as low a profile as possible. He told himself that eventually, the new kid effect would fade. People would stop noticing him. He'd become just another face in the crowd—ignored, overlooked. Even the teachers would struggle to remember his name. Like always. In the meantime, he kept himself busy, scribbling in his little idea notebook. He tried to design prototypes, just like in the good old days. He sent photos to his old friends, who replied with sketches of their own. It wasn't the same. It felt lonely and frustrating, but it was better than nothing.

Suddenly, during the break between two history lessons, a soft voice interrupted his thoughts.

"Hey, you're Miles, right? I'm Lena. I saw you drawing. It's cute... But, uh... What exactly is it? What are you working on?"

Terrified, Miles stammered something about a solar-powered, three-seater electric bike.

"Wow! Does that actually exist?"

"Not yet, but I'd love to build one."

"That's such a cool idea! I love it!"

"Really...? Do you draw too?"

"Yeah, but more like manga characters—not really the same kind of thing as you."

"Let me see..."

Lena—the prettiest girl in the class, a tall blonde with bright, playful eyes—handed him her notebook. Inside, he saw figures with spiky hair and vibrant, multicolored outfits. He had never read manga, but one character looked familiar.

That's Naruto, right...?"

Lena burst out laughing.

"Well, obviously! Is it that badly drawn?"

"No, no! Not at all, I just don't know much about it, that's all. Sorry..."

He was going to look like a total fool. No doubt about it. Once again, he was going to stand out without even trying. And if the teasing started with someone as popular as Lena, he was as good as dead. But instead, she immediately replied:

"Who cares! What you're doing is way more interesting. You're not just copying, at least!"

Lena looked at him with admiration. Unbelievable. She seemed genuinely interested in his technical drawing—a sort of taxi bike with a massive solar panel on top. She added eagerly:

"Do you draw a lot of these? Can I see the rest of your notebook?"

Class had started again, but the two of them were so caught up in their conversation that they didn't even notice. The teacher called them out, a little sharply, and told Lena to return to her seat. She flashed Miles a big smile and whispered discreetly as she walked away.

— *Beating Shyness with Talent!* —

"Meet me at lunch, okay?"

Two guys sitting nearby overheard the invitation. At first, they laughed. But their expressions quickly darkened. Who did this new kid think he was, flirting in class? Jake and Tyler weren't exactly the brightest of the bunch. Two hulking troublemakers who racked up detention hours like trophies and loved to trip people in the hallways... But Miles didn't notice a thing.

At lunch, Lena grabbed Miles's arm and hurried him toward the cafeteria. No way were they wasting twenty minutes standing in line. They walked in silence—Miles staring at the floor, Lena beaming as always. Once they sat down, the conversation picked up again.

"What if we drew together? You could teach me how to sketch machines, and I could add some color to your designs. What do you think?"

The poor boy didn't know where to put himself. Between the clatter of plates, the shouting all around, and all the eyes that seemed to be on them, he felt like he was about to faint. He barely managed to stammer a weak "good idea," which his new friend hardly even heard, too excited about the idea of their collaboration.

"I'm so tired of doing nothing on weekends. We could have drawing sessions!"

She was inviting him to hang out. Miles, who had never spent

— Beating Shyness with Talent! —

time alone with a girl before, felt his legs go weak. He might have been able to hide his nerves, if not for the two class bullies who suddenly dropped into the seats beside them without any warning.

"So, lovebirds, how's it going?"

"Chatting like a cute little couple, huh?"

"Lena, going for charity work now? Thinking of adopting a kid?"

"Look how shy he is. Makes you wanna pinch his cheek..."

"...or kiss him! I get it, Lena."

"Don't worry, new kid, we'll take care of you too!"

Lena ignored them completely, calmly cutting into her chicken kiev as if she hadn't even heard their taunts. Miles, on the other hand, felt his shame slowly morph into anger. For once, life was going his way. Lena was beautiful, smart, kind—and she was interested in him. This kind of chance probably wouldn't come again. He had to do something. Now.

"Get lost, you idiots!"

Stunned silence. Lena froze, her fork hovering mid-air. Jake and Tyler stood there, mouths slightly open. Clearly, no one had ever talked back to them like that. They exchanged a look, then got up and disappeared.

Victory! Or... maybe not. It only took a few seconds for Miles to notice the shift around him. No more glasses clinking against tables. No more shouts from hungry students. Something was happening. And Miles was at the center of it. He had just yelled at the school's biggest bullies. And the entire cafeteria had heard it.

He clenched his fists under the table, his nails digging into his palms. Lena, however, didn't move. She simply sat there, as if fully grasping the weight of what had just happened.

Slowly, the cafeteria noise returned, like an old machine sputtering back to life. Lena turned to Miles with a warm, knowing smile.

"Don't worry, they'll leave you alone eventually. They're just not used to people standing up to them."

Miles nodded hesitantly, but deep down, he knew this was only the beginning of his troubles. At the end of lunch, he parted ways with Lena, promising to meet up after school to draw together.

The afternoon dragged on endlessly. Miles couldn't stop thinking about the consequences of his outburst. He knew Jake and Tyler wouldn't just let it slide—they would want revenge. The looks they shot him during class only confirmed his fears. He had won a battle. But the war was far from over.

— *Beating Shyness with Talent!* —

After the bell signaled the end of classes, Miles hurriedly gathered his things. Lena was waiting for him by the gate. He joined her, heart pounding, and they walked away together, throwing a few nervous glances over their shoulders.

"Don't worry, Miles, they won't do anything when we're together," Lena reassured him. "Come on, let's go to my place. My mom's not home this afternoon—we'll have the house to ourselves."

They walked quickly, just in case. Once inside, Lena led him to her room—a bright, spacious space covered in manga and anime posters. Miles felt a little more at ease when he noticed a dedicated drawing corner, neatly arranged with pencils, markers, and sketchbooks. She gestured for him to sit down.

"Show me what else you've drawn."

They spent the afternoon exchanging ideas and sketches. Miles was impressed by Lena's talent for drawing characters, while she was fascinated by his futuristic machine designs. They experimented with a few combined drawings—Miles adding mechanical elements to Lena's characters. The results made them burst into laughter.

Their growing bond gave Miles a little more confidence. For the first time, he felt that maybe—just maybe—he could find his place in this new school. But that fragile sense of security shattered when Lena suggested they go out to buy some snacks.

— *Beating Shyness with Talent!* —

The moment they stepped outside, they spotted Jake and Tyler waiting at the corner. The two boys approached, smirking. Lena saw them too and instinctively grabbed Miles's hand, as if to shield him.

"So, new kid, you think you're some kind of big shot now?"

Lena stepped in, her voice firm.

"Leave him alone, Jake."

Tyler flashed a menacing grin.

"Oh, we just want to talk, that's all. Right, Jake?"

Miles felt fear creeping up, freezing him in place. Lena stepped in front of him, shielding him like a human barrier.

"You two are pathetic. He hasn't done anything to you."

The two boys exchanged a knowing glance. Before Miles could react, Tyler grabbed him by the collar and shoved him against the wall. Lena let out a cry of protest, but Jake held her back.

"Listen, new kid," Tyler murmured in a low, threatening voice. "If you want to survive here, you'd better learn your place. Got it?"

Miles, breathless, nodded. Tyler let go of him abruptly, and Miles collapsed to the ground. Jake released Lena, who

— *Beating Shyness with Talent!* —

immediately rushed to help him up. The two boys walked away, laughing.

"Are you okay?" Lena asked, worried.
Miles nodded, but tears were rising to his eyes. He felt humiliated and powerless. Lena led him inside her house, and they remained silent for a moment. Yet, the young girl didn't seem willing to let it get to her.

"Listen, Miles, you can't let them do this to you. You have to fight back. Show them you're not afraid!"

Miles bit his lip and admitted his confusion, avoiding her gaze.

"But how?! They're stronger than me..."

"We'll find a way. Together."

In the days that followed, Miles carefully avoided Jake and Tyler, but the idea of standing up for himself began to take root. Lena kept encouraging him, and they continued drawing together, imagining incredible machines. Their drawing sessions became precious moments, and Miles gradually found a sense of calm again.

One Friday, as they worked on a new project in Lena's garden, she suddenly made a surprising suggestion.

"What if we showed our drawings to everyone? We could organize a small exhibition at school. What do you think?"

— *Beating Shyness with Talent!* —

Miles hesitated.

"Do you really think anyone would be interested?"

"Of course they would! Our drawings are amazing. And besides, it could be a chance for you to show everyone who you really are..."

Miles felt both a wave of panic and a glimmer of hope. Maybe Lena was right. Maybe this was the moment to step out of the shadows.

The following weeks were spent preparing for the exhibition. Miles and Lena worked tirelessly, selecting their best drawings and getting them ready for display. Lena took charge of convincing the art teacher to let them use a room for the event. On the day of the exhibition, Miles felt nervous but excited. To avoid any risks, he had chosen not to invite his parents. Their presence might feel infantilizing, something that could hand more ammunition to the enemy. Lena and he had arranged their works on panels, creating a fascinating visual journey that blended technical sketches with manga characters.

The students began to gather, drawn in by the announcement of the exhibition. Miles stayed in the background, observing their reactions. To his surprise, many seemed genuinely interested. They stopped in front of the drawings, asked questions, and gave compliments. Even the teachers came by, congratulating Miles and Lena on their work.

Jake and Tyler made their entrance. Miles tensed, expecting another confrontation. But this time, they simply looked at the drawings, visibly impressed. Lena ignored them completely, focused on welcoming the visitors.

By the end of the day, Miles felt a new sense of pride rising in him. He had managed to showcase his talent, to stand out in a positive way. Lena joined him, smiling.

"See? Talent is meant to be shared!"

Miles looked at her with gratitude. Thanks to her, he had found the courage to come out of his shell. He knew the road ahead would still be long, but he felt ready to face whatever came next, with Lena by his side.

They left the school together, hearts light, already talking about their next projects. Miles now understood that even in a new environment, he could make friends and carve out a place for himself. He just had to believe in himself and never give up on his passions.

The Rules of Love

—— The Rules of Love ——

Like every morning, Gabriel sat at his desk, staring at his reflection in the small mirror hanging before him. A ritual. A ritual that grew harder each day, more unsettling. Now in his first year of Jefferson High School, he found himself wrestling with questions that felt overdue. *These things are usually figured out in middle school*, he kept telling himself.

His messy brown hair framed a gentle face, where uncertainty and hope intertwined. Gabriel carried the weight of his turmoil. He was still the boy with kind eyes, the one most people liked instinctively, but a veil of sadness was becoming harder to conceal. Each morning, the pressure seemed to build. Each morning, he wondered when freedom would finally come.

He felt attracted to girls—but also to boys. And that duality unsettled him. Who could he talk to? At home, no one. His parents, though loving, were deeply conservative. Sunday mass, traditional values, offhand remarks about "differences" in movies—any kind of open conversation was unthinkable. His father, a devout Catholic, never stopped preaching about the importance of the traditional family against a society that was falling apart, while his mother, though gentler, shared the same beliefs. Gabriel had once tried to bring up the topic, but the conversation quickly veered into outdated moral lectures. He had learned his lesson. No support would come from that side. Loneliness among his own. Pain.

Fortunately, there was Fatoumata. Originally from Senegal, she was his rock. From the moment they met in their sophomore year, a strong friendship had formed. Fatoumata had faced her own battles against prejudice and the stereotypes tied to her culture. They understood each other instinctively. With her, Gabriel could say anything—without fear of judgment.

That day, during their lunch break, Gabriel met Fatoumata under their favorite tree. It was a large oak at the far end of the courtyard, with a bench placed beneath it. Covered in graffiti and scarred with deep carvings, it wasn't much to look at, but it was *their* spot—a quiet place where their most personal conversations could stay secret.

"Something's wrong, Gabe, isn't it?"

"I... I don't know, Fatou. Sometimes, I wonder if I'm normal."

"What are you even talking about?!"

He hesitated, scanning the area to make sure no one was listening. All around him, Gabriel saw laughter, ease, the carefree energy of students unwinding after class—while inside, a knot was tightening in his stomach.

"I'm still attracted to both girls and boys. And I can't figure out who I really am. It's not going away. At home, I can't say anything. And if I talk about it here, I'm done for..."

Fatoumata nodded silently, her eyes fixed on the glass wall of the teachers' lounge in the distance. A long minute passed before she finally broke the silence.

The Rules of Love

"You know, Gabe, there's no such thing as 'normal' in love. What matters is what you feel. And what you feel is always valid. No one can challenge what's in your heart. Let people think what they want."

Gabriel sighed. He knew how lucky he was—to have a true friend, someone who understood him. His burden felt just a little lighter. She was right, of course. Deep down, he knew it. But the fear of mockery and rejection still loomed over everything.

They spent the rest of the break chatting about anything and everything. Fatoumata did her best to make her best friend smile. She told him about her own struggles at home and how she turned them into jokes. "You have to laugh, laugh, and laugh some more," she kept saying.

"If I can navigate between two completely different cultures, you should be able to navigate between your two desires…"

Her words struck a chord with Gabriel. She was right. Nothing was ever easy for anyone. After all, even straight love stories in movies and novels were filled with obstacles. If there were rules to love, who was to say anyone really knew them?

The following weekend, Gabriel went to visit his aunt Abigail. Unlike his parents, and despite her age, she was a very modern, open-minded woman. Though they had never directly discussed the subject, Gabriel knew she had sensed his unease. Maybe he would find the opportunity to talk to her about it... After all, as valuable as Fatoumata's words were, they were still those of a teenager who didn't know much about love. Not knowing any adults who belonged to that mysterious community called LGBTQ+, he saw Abigail as the only person he could turn to about these troubling attractions.

She lived in a small house on the outskirts of town. Her garden was a peaceful haven, filled with colorful flowers with names impossible to pronounce and neatly trimmed shrubs, carefully tended by Mr. Benson, her neighbor. Gabriel loved spending entire afternoons there, most often glued to his phone—much to Abigail's despair. Yet, in that place, he felt at peace, as if he belonged. His aunt adored having him over, and more often than not, he surprised her with unannounced visits. She would grumble out of principle, saying she wouldn't have time to cook him a proper meal, but he knew nothing made her happier than his spontaneous drop-ins.

This time, though, he couldn't hide his sadness. As she poured him a glass of lemonade, she spoke in her usual gentle voice.

"Gabriel, you know you can talk to me about anything, don't you?"

He froze. Abigail had a sixth sense, there was no doubt about it. The exact words he had been waiting for, at exactly the right moment.

"Yeah, I know, Auntie..."

―― *The Rules of Love* ――

"We're not always sure we're on the right path, and that's normal. No one ever truly knows who they are or what's best for them. But one thing's for sure—you're not alone."

More than ever, Gabriel felt the comforting warmth of this place. His aunt offered him a space of unwavering support. She didn't push him to speak, but he knew she would be ready to listen when he was ready to talk.

Like with Fatoumata, their conversation soon drifted to lighter topics—his future studies, his friends. And from it all, one simple yet powerful idea emerged, a phrase both wonderful and reassuring: "Follow your passions and stay true to yourself."

Having support was good. It was reassuring. But it wasn't enough. Gabriel needed to accept himself for who he was, and something was still missing. He had to open up to others, to step out of his bubble of secrecy.

One afternoon, on a whim, he gathered his courage and knocked on the door of Mrs. Castelli, the school's guidance counselor.

"Come in, come in!"

His throat tightened. A moment of doubt.

"Ah! Gabriel, it's been a while! What brings you here?"

"I need to talk to someone. About something... personal."

"I get the feeling this isn't about career guidance..."

"It isn't."

"Well then, this sounds serious. I'm listening. Take a seat and take your time."

Gabriel took a deep breath and let it all out—his doubts, his fears, his inability to talk to his parents. Mrs. Castelli listened intently, without interrupting, her eyes filled with understanding. It was as if she had expected this, or perhaps she heard confessions like this every day. Yet, when she finally spoke, it was only to say a few simple words.

"This is a big step you've taken today, Gabriel. I'm going to give you some contacts for support groups where you can meet other young people like yourself. It's important that you have a space to talk and realize you're not alone."

The following months were a time of discovery and transformation. Gabriel attended meetings for a group recommended by Mrs. Castelli, where he met other teenagers going through similar experiences. They shared their stories, their fears, and their hopes. More than anything, they built a close-knit, supportive community.

During these meetings, he met Julian, a boy his age who helped him see things from a new perspective. Julian had also struggled to accept his bisexuality, and their friendship quickly became a source of comfort for Gabriel. Along with Fatoumata, they formed a strong trio where laughter once again had its rightful place.

Fatou, always by his side, encouraged him at every step. One day, as they walked through the park next to the school, she said:

"I'm so proud of you. You've found the strength to accept yourself. I never doubted you would, but it's still a huge victory."

She smiled at him, and they continued walking side by side.

His parents, meanwhile, had started noticing changes in him. They didn't yet know the reason, but they saw their son looking more at peace, more fulfilled. Gabriel knew that one day he would tell them, but for now, simply feeling at ease with himself was more than enough.

The First Time…

— *The First Time...* —

At sixteen, Emma spent her days going to class, doing homework, and hanging out with friends—a typical teenage routine. But for the past three months, something new had shaken up her routine—something with a deep voice, irresistible eyes, and stubble on his chin: Adam. Their relationship was sweet, innocent, built on a deep connection. They had met in the school cafeteria while waiting for one of those dreadful sandwiches, and from that moment on, they had been inseparable. Intense gazes, laughter, and sometimes, tender kisses. Very long kisses... Everything was perfect. Or was it? A vague uneasiness gnawed at Emma, a quiet, lingering doubt that made her hesitate every time she was supposed to spend an afternoon at Adam's place.

Emma felt nervous about taking the next step in their relationship. Their conversations were filled with unspoken promises, but she couldn't shake the question looming in her mind—was she really ready to go further? She even considered breaking up with him, despite how deeply she cared for him. Leaving him, just to avoid disappointing him... A cruel dilemma.

While her friends spoke freely about their experiences, completely at ease with the topic, Emma kept her worries to herself. Yesterday, Ava bluntly asked her the inevitable question:

"And you, Emma, how are things with Adam?"

"Good! We get along really well."

―― *The First Time...* ――

"Have you two... you know, taken the next step?"

"Uh... No... Not yet..."

Ava exchanged a knowing glance with the two other girls, Emily and Brooke. Suddenly, Emma felt very alone.

When she got home, she sat at her desk, her mind racing. She opened her journal and began to write.

Dear Diary,

Why is everything so complicated? Adam is perfect, caring and patient. But every time someone makes a sexual comment around us, I feel a wave of panic. What if I'm not ready?

I'm scared I won't be good enough, that I won't know what to do. What if I disappoint him? Would he still love me? Or would he turn to girls who have already done it? I don't think Adam is like that, but people always say men only think about one thing. What if he ends up being like the others?

Maybe he'd even be right...

And once again, I ended up looking like a little kid. That idiot Ava, pretending she doesn't know I'm freaking out—just to make me admit I haven't done it. Now I feel pressure from both sides...

Emma

— The First Time… —

She had to talk to Adam about her worries. They met at the big park, their favorite place to walk together. Sitting on a bench, fidgeting nervously with the silver wrapper of the biscuits she had barely managed to eat, Emma decided to speak up.

"Adam, I... I need to talk to you about something important."

"You're scaring me... What's wrong? Did I do something stupid?"

"No, it's about our relationship... I feel... anxious about taking things further."

Adam took her hand in his. He looked relieved, almost glad that she had brought it up.

"Emma, I understand. We don't have to rush. We'll do it when you're ready. And, you know, it's true that I think about it too, that I want it, but I'm not exactly confident either. Guys are supposed to take the lead with these things, but I don't have any more experience than you do. I want us to take our time too."

She felt more loved than ever. For several days, she floated on a little cloud. But gradually, the situation began to change.

Adam, even though he had clearly reassured her that there was no pressure, started to behave a little more insistently. He made subtle remarks when inviting her over, and his hands wandered more than usual when they kissed. As if his

— *The First Time...* —

mind was reasonable, but his body was waiting. In spite of himself.

As if his mind was reasonable, but his body was waiting. In spite of himself.

Without really blaming him, she still felt a deep discomfort. Worse than before. She started thinking about the concrete reasons why the idea of having sex troubled her and wrote them down in her journal:

1. Fear of pain: What if it hurts?
2. Fear of not being good enough: What if I don't know what to do?
3. Risk of pregnancy: Even with precautions, that fear lingers.
4. Social pressure: Feeling like I have to do it just because everyone else is.
5. Impact on the relationship: What if things change between Adam and me afterward?

There were a lot of reasons. She wasn't crazy. Maybe anxious, maybe overly so, but not crazy—having sex, especially for the first time, was no small thing. And was Adam really the right one? That was another big question. Maybe she needed more time to think. After all, you only get one first time...

Her decision was paradoxical: to make no decision at all. One thing at a time. One step at a time. For now, she would focus on her studies, her friends, and enjoying the moments she shared with Adam—free from overthinking the future.

— *The First Time...* —

She would savor his presence, have a good time together, and stop projecting ahead. They would see where things went...

One evening, after watching a movie on Adam's tablet, lying shoulder to shoulder on his bed, he turned to look at her tenderly. Afraid that he might become too forward, she took the initiative:

"What?" she asked, narrowing her eyes. "Why are you looking at me like that?"

"You're beautiful, that's all."

"Oh, come on. I know you've got something on your mind..."

"Yeah, so what? Am I not allowed to?"

"I don't know..."

"Do I have the right or not?"

"You have the right to think about it, sure. But..."

"But what? Relax, I'm not going to jump on you if that's what you're afraid of!"

"I know... but still..."

"Still what?"

— *The First Time...* —

"I just know you think about it a lot, and I worry that you're getting too frustrated."

"Nah, we said we'd take our time, remember? Don't stress about it."

"Thank you, Adam..."

"You don't have to thank me. You're beautiful, I look at you, I want you, but I'm not an animal. I like you just as much as before. More, actually."

"I like you too. A lot. And I know I want to do this with you. I just need to be sure it's the right time, that I won't regret it, that's all."

At her last words, Adam's expression shifted. He closed off a little, saying nothing as he got up to grab his phone charger. Standing by the window, he stared outside. Emma immediately realized she had been clumsy with her words.

Dear Diary,

I can be so useless sometimes. Adam was an angel—he complimented me, reassured me. And what do I do? I blurt out that I don't want to regret it. He must have taken it as me doubting whether he's the right person, and now he's shut down over it. I have no idea how to fix this. At the same time... it's not completely false. I'm not sure of anything.

Anyway, I'm living in hell! Emma

—— *The First Time...* ——

The next day was difficult. Adam pretended to act as usual, but it was clear something was on his mind. Emma kept thinking about the image of her boyfriend, standing still by the window, and a wave of sadness and guilt washed over her. During the break, she found him in the hallway and said:

"Adam, I'm sorry if I hurt you yesterday. I didn't mean to make you feel like I don't trust you or that I don't love you."

He turned his head toward her, his eyes dark, his features tense.

"I understand you. Really. But sometimes, I need to know that you want us too, that you believe in what we can become together. It's not just about sex. It's about our future, our relationship."

She took a deep breath. This time, she had to choose her words carefully.

"You're right. I want us, and I want what we can become together. I want you too. Maybe... maybe we could talk about my fears one of these days?"

Adam seemed calmer.

At the end of the day, just outside the school gates, he asked her:

"Go ahead, tell me everything!"

— *The First Time...* —

"It's a mix of so many things. Not doing things right, not reacting the way you'd want me to, suddenly freezing up, feeling pain, getting pregnant... I'm also scared that you'll change afterward, that you won't see me the same way anymore."

"Wow, all that!" Adam burst out laughing. "That's quite the list. Sorry, I had no idea you had so much weighing on you!"

"Yeah, well, you're the one who does all the heavy lifting."

"Oh, ha-ha, very funny. But seriously, I'm glad you told me all this. It makes a lot more sense now. Honestly, none of it is crazy, especially with everything we hear around us."

"Really?"

"Of course. We'll go through it point by point and see what we can do."

"You're the best, I love you so much!"

"I love you too! But seriously, you could talk to your mom about it too, right? That's what moms are for!"

"That's kinda tough..."

"Come on, Emma, you're 16. I bet she's just waiting for you to bring it up."

─── *The First Time…* ───

That evening, as she found herself alone in the kitchen with her mother, Emma admitted that she wanted to talk about something very personal. Without even looking up from her mixing bowl, her mother immediately smiled.

"It's about Adam and me. We've been together for a few months now, and I'm wondering if I'm ready to take things further with him."

Her mother set down her knife and sat across from her.

"You know, there's no universal answer to that question. Every relationship is unique. The only truth is in your heart. When you're ready, you'll know. The most important thing is to never do this kind of thing for others. You do it with someone, but you do it *for* yourself."

Emma felt a tear roll down her cheek.

"I know, but it's so complicated. I'm scared of messing everything up."

Wiping away her tear, her mother assured her that if Adam was the right one, he would wait as long as needed. She also reminded her that, no matter how she might feel, their relationship was still quite new.

"There are couples who stay together for 50 years! Believe me, looking back, they know that waiting six more months wouldn't have made a difference."

— *The First Time...* —

These words resonated with Emma. And after all, things could indeed happen gradually.

The following night, she met her boyfriend in the large park. It was one of their little secrets: they would meet up after closing time, climb over the fence, and lie down on Adam's old blanket, gazing up at the stars. Sometimes, they would stay there for long stretches without saying a word, yet without feeling the slightest discomfort. True relationships, after all, could be measured by their silences—the ability to simply be next to each other, without the need for words. Just feeling the other's presence and finding happiness in it. These were wonderful moments, always ending with a double dose of stress. First, the challenge of sneaking back home without their parents noticing—no easy task! And then, the realization that, with the night so far gone, they'd barely get any sleep. They knew they'd be exhausted at school the next day, but even that became a source of laughter when they crossed paths in the hallways, dark circles under their eyes.
That evening, without any warning, it suddenly began to rain. At first, just a few heavy drops, but within moments, it turned into a full downpour. Laughing, they dashed under the gazebo, huddling together beneath the blanket. After a few minutes, still smiling, Adam asked with a hint of concern:

"What are we going to do if the rain doesn't stop?"

"Hmm..."

"What?"

— *The First Time...* —

"I have an idea..."

Emma gave him a mischievous look that Adam had never seen before. Was she actually suggesting that their first time could happen here, in the middle of a public park, under a gazebo? Unbelievable!

"Wait... Are you serious?"

"Let me think about it..."

"No, but seriously?!"

"Of course not, you idiot! Who do you think I am?"

And just like that, she burst into laughter, feeling an immense sense of relief. Playing along, even for just a few seconds, had been a challenge—but strangely, it had also freed her. She could feel it. While the idea of actually doing anything here had never been on the table, joking about it had completely eased her anxiety. Adam, too, seemed lighter.

"I swear, if I had insisted a little, you would have done it. You've got that look... You're completely crazy!"

"What are you doing after class tomorrow?"

"I'm inviting my girlfriend over!"

"She'll come... But without the rain."

Matthew the Liar

―― *Matthew the Liar* ――

At first glance, he's an ordinary boy. Plain, the kind who blends in, unnoticed. The type you only really register a week or two after school starts—or mistake for someone else.

On the surface, nothing set him apart. But beneath that unremarkable exterior, he had a rare skill, a sharp instinct that filled him with pride. Matthew was an exceptional liar. It came effortlessly, without planning, without hesitation. He lied—and he did it well.

From a young age, he had learned that truth was flexible, malleable—a soft clay he could shape however he pleased. Why present things in an unpleasant or unflattering light? Better to tell people what they wanted to hear or what suited him best. *That was the easiest way to keep life simple*, he told himself.

This story, a little absurd, is almost like a fable. It could begin around Matthew's fifth year, but instead, it starts on a Monday morning during his sophomore year, at exactly 8:10 a.m.

Matthew was late. His homeroom teacher, Mr. Mitchell, had his eyes fixed on the classroom clock when the teenager burst in, breathless, hair tousled. Instead of admitting he'd simply hit the snooze button one too many times, he declared in a firm, unwavering voice, "Sorry, Mr. Mitchell, I was attacked by a dog on my way here."

A stunned silence filled the classroom. Mr. Mitchell, a man usually strict but fair, raised an eyebrow, fixed his gaze on

— *Matthew the Liar* —

Matthew, and made no comment. The students exchanged skeptical glances, and the lesson resumed. Matthew felt that familiar rush of adrenaline he loved so much. *It's so easy*, he thought.

If the story begins with this episode, it's because it marks the start of a new phase, one where the boy began lying compulsively, almost against his own will.

In the following days, Matthew's lies became both more frequent and more outrageous. Didn't finish his math homework? His little brother spilled a glass of water all over his sheets—except he was an only child. Bombed his physics test? He had spent the entire evening trying to rescue a cat stuck in a tree in his garden—except he didn't have a garden…

His lies were met with a range of reactions. Some of his classmates started to doubt the truth of his stories, while others were intrigued, even impressed. As for the teachers, they were torn between sympathy and suspicion. *A strange boy, but not a bad one*, they thought.

But Matthew didn't stop there. He loved the attention his stories brought him. He told his friends that he had met MrBeast in a café, that he had discovered a treasure hidden in the wall of his grandmother's basement, and even that he had been approached for a role in a movie. Each lie seemed more incredible than the last. But since it kept working, there was no reason to stop. In fact, Matthew felt an exhilarating sense of power. Naturally, this couldn't last forever, and soon enough, unpleasant consequences began to unfold…

On a school trip, he pretended to be sick to avoid an activity he found boring. A museum?! No, thank you! Spending hours staring at old, uninteresting paintings… Hard pass. Concerned, Mr. Mitchell called his parents. Panicked, they rushed to the school, only to find their son in perfect health. He barely managed to talk his way out of it, claiming he had suffered a panic attack but overcame it using a breathing technique he had learned from a manga… His mother insisted on taking him to see a psychologist friend, but he dodged that too by saying he was drowning in schoolwork and that falling behind in biology would likely trigger another anxiety attack. She hesitated but eventually left him alone.

His friends, increasingly exasperated by his far-fetched stories, started distancing themselves. What once amused them now exhausted and unsettled them. It became impossible to tell when he was telling the truth or spinning another lie. He always had the same unreadable, impassive expression.

Did he realize it? Yes and no. He sensed that his antics didn't always land as expected, but he relished the thrill of deception just enough to keep going.

And then there was that terrible cycle of covering one lie with another, a trap he was slowly falling into. One evening, when he was supposed to be home early after going out with friends, he claimed to have witnessed a spectacular accident to justify his lateness. His parents, shocked, bombarded him

— *Matthew the Liar* —

with questions he no longer knew how to answer. He stammered, got tangled in his words, and began to worry that his father, who read the local newspaper religiously, might notice the absence of any mention of the incident. At dawn, he managed to sneak downstairs and hide the paper before anyone else could see it. But suddenly, he began to doubt his own talent for deception. And if there was one art that required unwavering confidence, it was lying.

Moreover, his school performance began to suffer. His teachers, tired of his constant excuses, stopped giving him the benefit of the doubt. They became stricter, demanding proof for everything he claimed. Matthew soon found himself trapped, unable to back up his far-fetched stories with real facts.

Bit by bit, he ended up alone. His friends drifted away, exhausted by his endless fabrications. His parents trusted him less and less, keeping a closer eye on him and questioning everything he said. His isolation became undeniable. He wandered through the school hallways, solitary, ignored by his classmates. His parents, at a loss, no longer knew how to help him. They had tried reprimanding him, reasoning with him, but nothing seemed to work.

One evening, as she came to pick him up from school, his mother took the opportunity to discreetly question Yan, one of Matthew's old friends whom she hadn't seen in a long time. She asked if there was a problem. He answered without hesitation:
"Matthew is a liar."

— *Matthew the Liar* —

As he wandered alone through the park, eager to escape the inquisitive stares of his parents, Matthew had an unexpected encounter. He ran into Lucas, a former classmate who had moved away the previous year. Once a close friend, Lucas was surprised to see Matthew in such a state. They lay down on the grass and started talking.

For the first time in a long while, Matthew felt compelled to tell the truth. He confessed to Lucas how he had become trapped in his own lies, how he had lost his friends and the trust of those around him. Lucas listened attentively, without judgment, and finally said:

"You know, it's never too late to change. People can forgive, but you have to be honest. With them, but even more so with yourself."

His words struck a chord. Deep down, what Matthew had always enjoyed was the challenge—the thrill of pulling off things most people wouldn't dare attempt. Lying all the time was, in a way, a performance. But stepping back, owning up to his mistakes, and trying to rebuild trust—that was a challenge just as great.

After all... given how far things had gone, it would have been sheer recklessness to keep going down the same path. He would change. He would earn back the trust of those he had let down!

The next day, at the end of class, Matthew gathered his courage and went to Mr. Mitchell's desk. He confessed

Matthew the Liar

everything—the imaginary dog, the missing homework, every lie he had told. Mr. Mitchell, though surprised by such a sudden shift in attitude, appreciated his honesty and gave him a second chance. He also promised to mention it to his colleagues at the next staff meeting.

Motivated by this experience, he went to each of his friends, confessing the truth and apologizing for his lies. He was ashamed. Most of the time, he kept his head down, his words barely audible, almost whispered. Some were receptive and understanding, while others were not. He knew that the road to redemption would be long, but it was part of the process he had chosen to begin.

Over time, things started to improve. His grades got better, his relationships with friends and family stabilized. Matthew realized that, even though telling the truth could be difficult, it was always the best choice.

However, a moral dilemma quickly arose. He was invited to Daniela's surprise birthday party. In itself, this was great news—he was finally reintegrating into group outings. But there was a catch: he had to keep it a secret, pretend to have forgotten her birthday, and hide in her room to surprise her on the big day. It was a lie. And Matthew had sworn never to go down that path again. He brought it up with Maddie, the organizer, who didn't understand his hesitation at all and got defensive. She told him it was just a "lie by omission," that all he had to do was say nothing. Impossible. He felt like he was slipping back, like an addict suddenly tasting the substance that had once controlled him.

Matthew the Liar

For him, the lesson was clear. Any lie, no matter how tempting in the short term, only led to problems in the long run. He had learned to value honesty and sincerity, to appreciate relationships built on mutual trust. This surprise birthday party couldn't be a good idea.

Days passed, and he couldn't make up his mind. In the end, he decided to stick to his new resolutions and take an honest approach. So, he spoke to Daniela directly.

"Daniela, I know I'm not supposed to tell you this, but there's a surprise being planned for your birthday. I don't want to ruin the party, but I promised myself not to lie anymore, not even by omission."

Daniela, initially surprised, gave him a warm, emotional smile.

"Thank you, Matthew. That's really kind of you to tell me. I understand your dilemma."

On the day of the birthday, she pretended not to know anything, playing along for her friends. The party was a success. It was a pivotal moment for Matthew. Though he wasn't entirely satisfied with having betrayed Maddie's trust, he had just proven to himself that it was possible to be honest while still fully participating in social life.

As the weeks went by, Matthew kept moving forward on this path. He even made new friends, drawn to his authenticity. His parents, noticing his change in attitude, gradually relaxed and began to trust him again.

— *Matthew the Liar* —

Another important turning point came when Matthew faced a tricky situation in class. He had to present a group project in history, but one of his teammates, Thomas, hadn't done his share of the work. Instead of covering for him with a lie, as he once might have, Matthew chose to be honest:

"Mr. Mitchell, our project isn't complete because Thomas wasn't able to finish his part. We tried to help him, but we ran out of time. The whole group takes responsibility for it."

Once again, Mr. Mitchell appreciated Matthew's transparency and granted them an extra week.

Thomas, moved by Matthew's honesty and support, made up for it and did an excellent job. Not only was their project finished on time, but it also received a great grade!

The day after the final class council of the year, Mr. Mitchell called for everyone's attention before going over the individual grades and teacher comments:

"Among you, there is a student who has shown that we can overcome our flaws and become a better person. His journey is an inspiration to us all. No need to say his name, everyone has recognized him. Well done. Well done, and thank you."

Matthew was deeply moved. This was it, he had done it. He had truly changed.

In the following years, Matthew continued his studies with the same integrity and commitment. Every relationship he

— *Matthew the Liar* —

built was founded on trust and sincerity. He knew better than anyone that truth, though sometimes difficult to face, was the foundation of a fulfilling life. After graduating high school, he went on to study law. His friends teased him, saying he was bound to become a lawyer... An ironic career choice for someone who had sworn to always tell the truth.

He usually just smiled without answering. Deep down, he had no doubt. He would become a judge. Finding and upholding the truth—that would be his life's work.

As Ugly as a Toad

— *As Ugly as a Toad* —

Kevin had always struggled with his body image. At 14, he felt more miserable than ever. He spent hours in front of the mirror, agonizing over every flaw he could see—his cheeks too round, his stomach slightly chubby, his arms too thin. At school, he hid under baggy clothes, hoping to go unnoticed.

Puberty had been a real upheaval. Hair sprouted under his arms and on his face. A sudden, dramatic growth spurt. His voice cracked. In short, he had gone through a physical transformation like every boy his age—but, unlike every boy his age, he experienced it as something uniquely intense.

While most of his friends were thrilled to see themselves turning into men, for him, it was just another reason to despise himself. "What's the point of having body hair if it grows in all the wrong places?" "My voice has changed, but I think it might actually be worse than before..." "If only my muscles had kept up with my bones stretching, I wouldn't look like this ridiculous lanky twig!" In short, nothing was right. Nothing was ever right. Deep down, Kevin saw himself as unattractive.

Whenever he caught his reflection in a car window or a shop display during walks with friends, the reality of his body would hit him all over again. And he felt ashamed. Ashamed of being so ugly. Ashamed of forcing others to endure his awkward presence.

Except Kevin wasn't ugly. In fact, most girls found him quite cute. He saw himself as a monster without ever considering that his self-perception might be completely out of sync with

—— As Ugly as a Toad ——

reality. The problem was, his shame ran so deep that he never spoke about it to anyone. Instead, he played the role of the confident guy, hiding beneath oversized skate clothes...

That year, Ms. Bradford, the art teacher, went from class to class announcing the launch of a new "Self-Esteem Workshop." She encouraged all students to give it a try, emphasizing that they didn't need to have confidence issues to join.

Quite the opposite, it'd be great to have all kinds of students participate, whether they struggle with confidence or not. It'll be a shared space for discussions, creative exercises, and fun activities. Honestly, isn't that better than just hanging around the courtyard doing nothing during lunch?"

A solid argument, especially with the freezing weather. Kevin only knew Ms. Bradford by reputation. People said she was kind and funny, not overly academic. Some even called her "crazy," but if you listened to students, every teacher was a little crazy. Kevin found the idea appealing. He mentioned it to his seatmate, Jenna—a stunning brunette with curly hair whom he had secretly loved since middle school. She was his "best friend." She adored Kevin and confided in him constantly, never suspecting how he truly felt.

It didn't really matter—Kevin handled it well. He promised himself that one day, he would tell her everything, but for now, he had to keep up appearances. There was no way he'd bring up how much he hated his own body. In his mind, Jenna could already see how unattractive he was, so there was no point in making her pity him even more by whining about it.

On the other hand, Jenna often opened up about how she was feeling. Getting her first period had been a nerve-wracking experience. Sure, it was a sign of maturity, and she was excited about becoming a woman, but it also brought a lot of confusion. She had warned Kevin in advance and even apologized for the emotional changes she might go through. Their biology teacher had explained how hormonal fluctuations could cause mood swings or make people extra sensitive.

This was the perfect opportunity.

"You know what, Jenna? If you're up for it, I'll go with you. This thing could actually be cool, don't you think?"

"Really? I was hoping you'd say that. Yeah, I'd love to go. I'm not feeling my best lately. But are you sure it won't bore you?"

"Of course not! And anyway, it's freezing outside these days. We'll be way more comfortable in there. Sound good?"

On the day of the workshop, the art classroom had been completely transformed. Colorful posters covered the walls with messages like "You are unique" and "True beauty comes from within." It was a bit cheesy, but maybe that's exactly what the participants needed to see and hear.

— *As Ugly as a Toad* —

That the participants needed to see and hear. Ms. Bradford warmly welcomed each of them, explaining that this workshop would be a safe space where everyone could express themselves freely.

The first activity was to write a letter to themselves, something uplifting… Kevin, hesitant at first about the oddity of the exercise, finally picked up his pen and started writing. "Dear Kevin," he began, "I know you struggle to love yourself as you are. But remember, everyone has their flaws. You are kind, funny, and intelligent. Your friends appreciate you for these qualities, not for your appearance." Not bad.

Then, Ms. Bradford organized a group exercise where each participant had to say something positive about the person next to them. Kevin, sitting beside Lily, a girl from his class whom he found intimidating, was taken aback when she looked him straight in the eye and said, "Kevin, you have an amazing sense of humor. You always make everyone laugh, even on tough days. You're actually super important!"

Her words struck him. He realized he had never considered that others might see beyond his appearance. One by one, the other members of the group did the same, and Kevin felt overwhelmed by the genuine and heartfelt compliments he received.

As the workshop went on, he grew more comfortable. They discussed media influence and how unrealistic beauty standards are portrayed. Ms. Bradford introduced a guest speaker, a young influencer who had struggled with body image himself and shared his inspiring story. He had come up with a brilliant title for his talk: "From Invisible in the Hallways to 15K on Instagram."

What struck Kevin the most was how the guy had perceived himself before his online success. He used to think he was hideous and had actually loved the lockdown period because it allowed him to hide behind a mask:

"I think that was the most comfortable I've ever been in my life. No one could see my pointy chin or that awful smile anymore!"

He burst out laughing before continuing:

"The craziest part? There were actually a few girls at my school who said they had a crush on me. People would tell me, but I was convinced they were just making fun of me... At first, I started posting on Instagram as a kind of therapy, a way to accept myself physically. And the wildest thing? There were always people leaving compliments... I couldn't believe it. So, I started speaking up for everyone who looks in the mirror and hates what they see. And that's when I realized— there are so many of us. Truth is, people who are genuinely comfortable with their appearance? They're incredibly rare."

He paused, scanning the faces in the room, then added:

"Now, I'm one of those people."

Applause erupted from the group! It was an incredible

— *As Ugly as a Toad* —

testimony, full of strength and sincerity. Jenna had tears in her eyes.

By the end of the day, Kevin felt something shift inside him. For the first time, he considered the possibility of accepting himself as he was. Inspired by the workshop, he suggested to Jenna, Lily, and the other participants that they start a school-wide awareness campaign to promote diversity and self-acceptance. Ms. Bradford was thrilled!

They got to work right away, creating posters, organizing discussions, and sharing personal stories. Their campaign, titled "Unique and Proud", quickly gained traction. Students—and even teachers—got involved, sharing their own experiences and supporting the initiative.

The following days were filled with a new energy. Kevin, Jenna, Lily, and the other workshop participants met regularly to plan their campaign. Their discussions were lively, with everyone contributing ideas and sharing experiences to develop the project. Kevin felt more confident each day. By encouraging others to accept themselves, his own self-rejection gradually lost its grip. He started doing his hair in the morning with enjoyment and only noticed his small imperfections with a passing glance.

They decided to wrap up the campaign with a large assembly in the gymnasium. Fearing a low turnout, Ms. Bradford managed to convince the principal to make attendance mandatory for everyone! The school administration even helped them organize the afternoon.

— As Ugly as a Toad —

On the big day, the auditorium was packed with students and curious teachers. The walls were beautifully decorated, thanks to the help of the Art elective students. Everyone had contributed. Even better—each had given their very best. The atmosphere was charged with anticipation, but Kevin felt ready.

Lily spoke first, sharing her own struggle with self-acceptance, growing up in the shadow of two brilliant older sisters who were admired by everyone. She talked about how she had learned to see herself in a more positive light. Her honesty resonated with the audience, and Kevin noticed several heads nodding in understanding.

Then it was his turn. Heart pounding, he stepped onto the stage and took a deep breath. "Hey, everyone," he began, his voice echoing through the hall.

"I'm Kevin, and two weeks ago, I was as ugly as a toad!"

An awkward silence filled the room.

"Now, I think I'm not too bad. Right? What do you guys think?"

He began alternating between bodybuilder poses and high-fashion model stances. The entire room burst into laughter—not mocking laughter, far from it, but a genuine, hearty laugh. A laugh of surprise and relief, a shared moment of joy that celebrated the speaker's courage!

— *As Ugly as a Toad* —

A group of girls started chanting, "Kevin! Kevin! We love you!", mimicking concert fangirls. Grinning, he blew them kisses before shifting to a more serious tone. He spoke about his struggles with body image, the shame he had felt, and the loneliness that had often followed him. But he also shared how Ms. Bradford's workshop, the letter he had written to himself, and Lily's words had left a lasting impact on him.

"Sometimes, we are our own worst critic. I've learned that what others see in us can be completely different from what we see in ourselves."

Applause erupted, and Kevin felt a warmth spread through him. He went on to explain the goal of the "Unique and Proud" campaign.

"We want everyone here to feel accepted and valued for who they are," he declared. "Diversity is what makes us strong. Together, we can create a school where everyone feels welcome and appreciated."

He wrapped up with a final statement:

"Nobody's perfect, but that's the best part: nobody wants to be!"

Once again, thunderous applause filled the room.

The next day, the school was buzzing with energy. Everywhere Kevin went, he was met with smiles and words of encouragement. He could feel that something had shifted—not just within him, but all around him. The atmosphere at school seemed lighter, more supportive, more united.

Jenna and Kevin decided to extend the campaign. They set up weekly discussion groups where students could share their experiences and support one another. With the support of the school nurse and teachers from History, Geography, and Social Sciences, they also organized workshops on topics like the impact of social media, stress management, and self-confidence. Each session became a safe space where students could express themselves freely and support one another.

One day, as Kevin was leaving one of these workshops, he felt a hand on his shoulder. It was Lily, smiling shyly.

"Kevin, I just wanted to say that what you've done—for me and for everyone—is truly incredible. You've changed the way I see myself. Thank you."

Kevin was deeply moved by her words.

"Thank you, Lily. You've done a lot for me too. Without your comment that day at the workshop, I don't know if I would have had the courage to keep going."

She flashed him her brightest smile before darting off down the hallway. But after ten steps, she stopped. Turning back, they locked eyes, holding each other's gaze from afar. Then, with a final glance, Lily disappeared into the classroom.

Anorexia

— Anorexia —

My name is Mila. I'm a normal girl—or at least, as normal as anyone can be. For most of us, being a teenager is a real ordeal. You feel the world shifting, inside you and all around you. It's exciting, it's terrifying. But above all, it's hard.

For me, it was hell.

Anorexia.

It's a word that scares people. A word you barely hear, or only in passing. An eating disorder driven by an intense fear of gaining weight and a distorted perception of one's own body. Remember this: anorexia, often linked to low self-esteem, isn't just physical. It's primarily mental.

You should also know that anorexia and bulimia can be connected. Sometimes, a person struggling with anorexia may also experience binge-eating episodes. During these episodes, they consume an enormous amount of food in a very short time. Afterward, they often feel shame and guilt, leading them to purge—by vomiting, taking laxatives, or exercising excessively. It's a destructive cycle.

These disorders are complex and dangerous. You can't overcome them alone. I wanted to share my story, told like a fable. Why? Because any teenager could face this one day.

Let's talk about it without shame.

- - - - -

— *Anorexia* —

Mila is in her final year of high school. She juggles the expectations of her parents, her teachers, and, most of all, her friends. Social media only amplifies her insecurities. A single like, a single comment can shape her mood for the entire day. She feels the constant pressure to be perfect, like the girls she sees on Instagram — always slim, always smiling. But how do they do it? Mila searches, without finding, whatever it is she's missing to measure up. Measure up to what? She couldn't say.

In truth, social media is everywhere in her life. Every day, she spends hours scrolling, comparing her body to those of the girls on her screen. She knows the photos are edited, that the angles are carefully chosen by image experts, yet that doesn't stop the overwhelming feeling of not being enough. With every picture, she tells herself she could do better, be better.

For the past few months, an unease has been growing inside her. Not the kind that erupts into tears or screams, but a quiet anxiety that eats away at her from within. She stares at herself in the bathroom mirror, scrutinizing every imperfection, every inch of skin she wishes were different. By the middle of the school year, her thoughts have narrowed in on one thing... Her appearance.

In the high school hallways, she walks surrounded by her friends. They're chatting about the latest video from an influencer they all follow. Mila listens absently, her mind elsewhere. She's thinking about what she'll eat for lunch and how to avoid eating too much without anyone noticing. Her

— *Anorexia* —

friends are completely absorbed in their conversation, carefree. No one sees Mila crumbling inside. She's fading, little by little. She's slipping away from herself.

Mila gradually loses touch with reality.

At first, the changes in her eating habits were subtle. She skipped breakfast, claiming she wasn't hungry. At lunch, she stuck to a salad, saying she was on a diet. Her friends teased her playfully but didn't suspect a thing. In the evening, she only picked at her dinner under her mother's worried gaze. She was probably the only one who sensed that something was wrong. But she didn't say anything. As if she were afraid of the words. Afraid of the word. *Anorexia*.

Mila's thoughts became more and more obsessive. Every bite of food turned into a calculation, an inner battle. She weighed herself multiple times a day, searching for validation that the mirror refused to give her. Her grades started to slip, but she didn't care. Her body was her only concern. It was a vicious cycle, and things spiraled quickly.

She hid food in her room to avoid eating in front of her family. She woke up at night, starving, and sometimes gave in to bingeing, only to purge afterward. She is exhausted, physically and emotionally, but she can't stop. That's just how it is.

One afternoon after school, Mila is alone in her room. Hunger gnaws at her, but she fights not to give in. Her mind is a battlefield, every thought a poisoned arrow. She stands in

— Anorexia —

front of her mirror, inspecting every inch of her body. She pinches the skin on her stomach, frowning at what she sees as too much flesh, too much fat, too much of everything.

The mirror is a friend because it alone seems to reflect the truth. The mirror is an enemy because it reflects an image she cannot accept. A paradox with no escape.

That night, in a moment of desperation, she reaches under her bed for the cereal box she had hidden and begins to devour it frantically, almost in a trance. Each bite is accompanied by silent tears. She knows she won't be able to keep the food down. Within minutes, she rushes to the bathroom, heart pounding. Relief and guilt intertwine as she leans over the toilet, trying to rid herself of what she just consumed. Two fingers down her throat, and it's done.

When it's over, she slides down against the wall, exhausted, her body trembling. An empty feeling washes over her—physical and emotional. She knows she can't go on like this, but how can she escape this darkness inside her? Mila spends the rest of the evening locked in her room, refusing to come down for dinner. This time, a migraine is her excuse to avoid the worried looks.

Her friends start noticing her absence at lunch. They find her more distant, lost in her thoughts. Mila knows she's pulling away from them, but she feels powerless to break the cycle. Her weight becomes an obsession. Every pound lost is a victory, every pound gained a failure.

— *Anorexia* —

One day, in the middle of gym class, she collapses. The school nurse, alarmed by her condition, calls her mother. Mila is taken to the hospital for tests, and the diagnosis is severe: she has a serious eating disorder and needs immediate care.

Her family is devastated. Her mother, in tears, can't understand how she didn't see it coming. Mila, on the other hand, feels torn between shame and relief. She no longer has the strength to fight alone. This moment marks a turning point—she must now choose to fight for her life.

The road to recovery is long, painfully long. Mila is admitted to a specialized unit where she meets other young people like her. Like her, yet each with their own story, their own fears, their own demons. The first days are the hardest. Constantly monitored, with every meal controlled, she feels like she's in prison, serving a sentence. The only real difference is the mandatory therapy sessions. Every small victory is celebrated, warmly so, but setbacks are frequent and discouraging.

Mila meets Claire, another patient her age who has been hospitalized longer but seems more at peace. They quickly bond, becoming each other's pillars of support. Claire shares her own struggles, the moments of despair, and the small victories that kept her going. Together, they talk, laugh, and cry. Claire shows her that hope is not just necessary but possible—that each day is a new chance to heal. Recovery is not about rushing; it's about working with time. Time is the ground on which healing grows.

— *Anorexia* —

Therapy sessions, however, are exhausting. They require her to confront fears that are difficult to name, to understand where her distress comes from, and, most importantly, to learn to see herself differently. She discovers that her anorexia is tied to a multitude of factors: the need for control, societal pressure, low self-esteem, and buried traumas. Little by little, she learns to identify the triggers of her episodes and to express her emotions in ways other than through food restriction. In itself, that is already a huge step.

Her family becomes part of the healing process. It's not easy in such an intimate struggle, especially after keeping them at a distance for so long, but Mila quickly realizes that this kind of support — one she knows is unwavering — is essential. Her parents attend family therapy sessions, where they learn to understand the illness, talk about it, and create a safe environment for their daughter. These are particularly difficult moments for everyone, but they help rebuild stronger, more lasting bonds that go beyond the illness.

Is that enough? No, of course not. The urge to regain full control returns. Just like before. But was it really worse before? Yes, obviously, but when you're suffering, you lack clarity — especially when the battle is against yourself. There are still many days when she looks in the mirror with disgust, with self-loathing. But she is learning to ask for help, to lean on her loved ones and the medical team. Every relapse is followed by a renewed sense of determination, a fresh start.

One of the turning points in her journey comes with the discovery of dance therapy. The goal is simple: to reconnect

— Anorexia —

with her body in a positive way. She lets herself be carried by the music, explores movement, and learns to appreciate what her body can do rather than how it looks. In fact, dance becomes a form of liberation, an outlet where emotions can be expressed without judgment.

Months go by, and Mila slowly begins to regain weight. The progress is gradual, but perhaps those are the most meaningful victories—the ones that cost the most. Her cheeks regain color, her eyes shine again. She starts smiling, laughing. The obsessive thoughts about food still linger in the background, but they become less overpowering. She learns to live with them, to strip them of the control they once had over her.

And then there's dance therapy, again and again. It becomes a language, a way to express what is too heavy to put into words. In the studio, surrounded by mirrors and music, she feels the strength of her body and the beauty of movement. Every dancer brings their own story, their own emotions. The rehearsals are intense, sometimes challenging, but also cathartic. Mila finds herself enjoying these moments of connection and creation. Within the group, she discovers an unexpected source of support—a solidarity that lifts her up. Bonds are formed, not through competition or judgment, but through acceptance and mutual encouragement. These are unspoken connections. Everyone has learned to communicate beyond words.

- - - - -

— *Anorexia* —

My name is Mila. I'm just a regular girl—which is to say, nothing about me is truly ordinary. For most of us, being a teenager is a real challenge...

But challenges shape us, strengthen us. Today, I stand before you, not as a victim, but as a survivor. Was my life harder than others? Harder than yours? I don't know. Many would probably say yes. But I believe that nothing is easy for anyone, and everything we overcome shapes us into the adults we become.

I'm not here to give lessons. Just an observation: no one gets through obstacles alone. You can try. Sometimes, you might even succeed. But sooner or later, the time comes to accept help. And trusting others—perhaps that's the best way to learn to trust yourself.

Finding Your Path

— *Finding Your Path* —

"Honestly, sir, I have no idea what I want to do. No point even trying to figure it out."

I knew that casually tossed-out phrase carried a lot of weight. Every year, I heard it in every class. Every year, I chose not to rush to reassure them. Students hate two things: being lectured and having their future talked about in a way that sounds too definitive. Yes, they'll figure it out. All of them. Some sooner, some later, but they'll all manage to "find their way"—since that's the phrase everyone uses. And no, they don't need to be constantly comforted with overused phrases and reassurances they can instinctively tell are worn out.

I teach philosophy. I work with two grade levels: seniors and juniors, for those who have chosen the Humanities, Literature, and Philosophy elective. I'm a teacher, but if there's one thing I don't care much about, it's the official curriculum. I prepare my students for their finals, but only as a side task. Just one part of the bigger picture. And that bigger picture is what really matters: life.

Don't get me wrong. No one expects a philosophy teacher to hand out reasons or instructions on how to live. That's not the point. My job is to deepen their experience of existence, to walk alongside them as they navigate their own paths. Nothing more, nothing less.

So when Jamal tells me he has no idea what he'll do with his life, I see it as a significant intellectual process in itself—he's experiencing his relationship with time. And that's exactly

— *Finding Your Path* —

what we start talking about.

"So what you're telling me is that you can't see the future, is that it?"

"No, I mean, I don't know what I want to do after high school."

"That's exactly what I'm saying—you're not a fortune teller. And does that bother you?"

"Well, I still have to fill out my college applications…"

"Like everyone else, Jamal. And they don't see the future any better than you do."

"Yeah, but the others already know what schools or universities they're going to apply to."

"They don't know anything. They assume. They imagine. They project. They fantasize. Sometimes, they even lie—just to get it over with. And honestly? They're probably right to do so!"

The system is designed in such a way that we're expected, at a very young age, to choose a path. So many roads stretch out before us. Today, new schools keep popping up, new specializations emerge. But, much like standing before an enormous dessert buffet, having options can be both exciting and overwhelming. Worse yet, sometimes nothing looks appealing at all. And yet, you're forced to choose. Parents, teachers, guidance counselors... The entire society chimes in. I know students are staring down their professional future, pushed toward it with an insistence that borders on bad taste. For Olivia, an outstanding student, the type who wants to excel at everything, things seem simpler:

"I'm going for a selective humanities prep program, then Harvard or Georgetown for political science, and after that, the Kennedy School, if I can pass the entrance exam. I'd like to work in a government department."

"Quite the plan!"

That's the kind of student I love. A powerhouse, a relentless machine that never questions itself... Until the moment it does.

I've seen so many of these brilliant students mapping out their prestigious paths to success. Most of the time, they hit a turning point. Maybe their grades suddenly slip in a key subject, or maybe life throws something unexpected their way. I remember Elena—a total all-star, top of her class in every subject from sophomore to senior year, destined to follow in her father's footsteps into the operating room. But she never made it past her third year of med school. Why? She discovered theater. It changed everything. The whole world tried to "talk sense into her," to put her back on the "right track," but it was pointless. Elena had swapped the surgeon's scalpel for stage costumes. Now, she scrapes by on small roles and still dreams of making it big. Every now and then, she sends me an email. She doesn't make much, but she doesn't complain—far from it. She's happy because she found herself. She's proud to have escaped the dreams her family had for her, those dreams that trap you, the kind you only break free from with an act of courage.

"You're ambitious, Olivia. That's great! But what is it about working in a government department that appeals to you? Serving your fellow citizens? The thrill of political life? Carving out a name for yourself to eventually become a public figure? And which department are you thinking of? Foreign Affairs? Health? Culture? The Economy? They're all very different…"

"I don't know yet; I find everything interesting."

"You see, Jamal? Olivia isn't much ahead of you either…"

Jamal didn't look convinced. I'm not surprised. In his eyes, Olivia was destined for success, if only because she was "a rich kid." But all I saw was a hard worker, and I couldn't help but feel frustrated by his reasoning. It was unfair to Olivia, dismissing all her effort just because she came from a well-off family. Some of my colleagues shared this kind of reverse social bias too. But it was just as unfair to Jamal. He saw the future as already set in stone, as if his path had been decided for him. He was blind to his own freedom. That's when I decided to shake things up a little.

"Imagine a waiter. He wears a crisp white shirt, a black vest, and has a neatly trimmed mustache. He moves swiftly between tables, takes orders, cracks a joke with the customer at the counter, greets a regular with warmth—all

— *Finding Your Path* —

while balancing his tray effortlessly in one hand. He's pleasant, skilled and professional. This example comes from the philosopher Jean-Paul Sartre, who draws an important conclusion from it: this is a waiter playing the role of a waiter."

The class didn't seem to follow me. I'm not surprised. So, I continued:

"He doesn't just perform the job he's expected to do. He is the role. He plays along so completely that it becomes his mask. His identity merges with his function, and every one of his actions is dictated by it."

Loris spoke up:

"Of course he is, he's a waiter."

"No! He's not. It's his job, not who he is."

"I don't get it."

"Loris, when you whine about a pop quiz, you're an 'acting student.' It means you're confusing yourself with your social role and limiting yourself to it. Sartre calls this bad faith."

"And what does that have to do with Jamal's plans…?"

"Well, Jamal plays the working-class kid just like Olivia plays the privileged one. They're both stuck in their roles. Both are showing bad faith by pretending they aren't free."

— Finding Your Path —

Naturally, remarks like these led to confusion, but so what? Part of my job was to provoke. If they got offended, all the better! It's through that discomfort that they might start questioning the roles imposed on them, the weight of family expectations. It's through that irritation that they might just begin to crave freedom. The world is full of Jamals and Olivias who believe themselves to be free individuals, when in reality, they're nothing more than social constructs.

Loris, back for more, tried to get back at me on behalf of his classmates:

"And you, sir, when you tell us to stop talking or to study our lessons, aren't you just a teacher playing the role of a teacher?"

"Well played, Loris! Exactly! I'm not mocking you—I fall into the same habits, the same bad faith. No matter how much we try to approach our jobs in our own way, the fact remains that true freedom comes at a price. I could tell you to skip class, that school isn't all that important. That would be my personal opinion, and I'd be sincere, but…"

"But…?"

"But I'd get fired! So I'd rather play the role of a teacher and, every now and then, try to pull you out of your own limiting roles. Jamal has the world at his feet—literally. Every step he takes is already a direction. And with each step, he gets to decide who he wants to be. Olivia has the same freedom, which means she could also let go of her grand ambitions, or

— *Finding Your Path* —

even choose a different kind of greatness. She's an incredible, brilliant girl, and all the effort she's putting in now will serve as keys to her future. Through hard work, she's expanding her freedom—let's just hope she knows how to use it!"

You won't be surprised to hear that, after this incident, I was summoned by the principal. Apparently, some parents didn't appreciate my methods… I was accused of categorizing my students based on their social class. What nonsense! It was exactly the opposite.

No, what I was really being criticized for was taking the pressure off career choices and, even worse, stripping them of parental influence. Parents are advisors. Caring, attentive advisors, yes, but advisors nonetheless. It's true that navigating delicate relationships with parents was never my strong suit—I preferred to speak directly to my students' critical thinking.

In short, I found myself in front of the principal, playing it humble.

"I'll be more mindful of how I phrase things from now on. But it's essential that students understand they're not confined by the social roles imposed on them…"

The principal gave a slight smile.

"I know that. That's precisely why you're here and not somewhere else. Your unconventional approach has its merits. But we also have to be mindful of sensitivities. Philosophy should illuminate, not blind."

"I'll do my best to find the right balance."

He nodded, satisfied, and took the opportunity to propose a small project.

"Perhaps you could organize interclass philosophical debates? It would be a good way to channel your students' energy into something constructive."

I liked the idea. Why not, after all, use these debates to explore themes of career choices, challenging them with different professional and existential perspectives?

We discussed the logistics for a while longer, then I headed back to class. The students were already waiting, eager to know what had been decided.

Loris was the first to speak, a hint of regret in his eyes.

"So, sir... Are you leaving us?"

I smiled, amused that word of my meeting had already spread throughout the school.

"No, of course not. And actually, I have a new idea for you. We're going to organize philosophical debates about career choices. You'll get to challenge each other's ideas, defend your viewpoints, and maybe even uncover perspectives neither you nor I had ever considered."

Jamal, still deep in thought, raised his hand.

"Sir, does that mean we'll have to speak in front of everyone?"

"That's right! Speaking in public is already a step toward finding your path. It means giving shape to your convictions and turning them into driving forces."

Olivia, on the other hand, already looked eager to shine in this new challenge.

The first debate took place the following week. The chosen topic was "The Importance of Academic Guidance in Shaping One's Identity."

Olivia kicked things off with a well-structured and passionate argument about the need to follow one's ambitions. Jamal, on the other hand, defended a more flexible and open approach, arguing that academic choices shouldn't confine individuals to definitive paths from a young age.

The debate was lively. At first hesitant, the students soon got into the rhythm, developing their ideas with growing confidence. I watched them, filled with pride, seeing the spark of critical thinking light up in their eyes.

At the end of the discussion, I spoke up:

—— Finding Your Path ——

"You see, choosing a path isn't a life sentence. It's a journey—one filled with decisions, discoveries, and possibilities. You are not locked into a single role. You have the power to change direction, to reassess your aspirations, and to shape your own path. There's no such thing as the wrong road."

The students seemed thoughtful, some even inspired.

One day, as I was grading papers in the teachers' lounge, I received an email from Elena, my former student. She shared how she had landed a small role in a promising theater production and thanked me once again for encouraging her to follow her passion.

I couldn't help but smile, thinking of Elena, Olivia, Jamal, and all the others. Each of them, in their own way, was carving out their path, exploring their possibilities. After all, my role was never to dictate a path but to guide them in their search for freedom and meaning. And to me, that was the greatest mission of all.

Courtney. Sixteen.
A Short Fuse

— *Courtney. Sixteen. A Short Fuse.* —

Courtney. Sixteen. A Short Fuse.

That should be enough to introduce myself. Seriously, teachers who make you fill out these "getting to know you" sheets at the start of the year are the worst. It was tolerable in middle school, but now? Just pointless. They never even read them. Honestly, I feel like writing total nonsense. In fact, I will.

Parents' Occupations

Dad: Serial killer
Mom: American rap star

Career Goals

Writing pointless introduction sheets for the rest of my life. Love it. Are there training programs for that?

Favorite Subject(s))

The cafeteria.

Sports I Play

Curling, MMA, Santa's sleigh racing.

There. We'll see if the homeroom teacher has a sense of humor. Honestly, he should thank me. After reading through all the fake, try-hard answers from everyone else, maybe he'll get a laugh out of mine.

— *Courtney. Sixteen. A Short Fuse.* —

He didn't laugh. Mr. Callahan (an absolutely meaningless name) called me in at the end of the next class. Apparently, he holds himself in too high regard to waste time on childish antics. Fine by me—I don't have time to waste either. Though, maybe I shouldn't have said that to his face…

You know my problem. No need to say more. I snap way too fast. Of course, people could say I'm too impatient, too extreme, too intolerant, too much of this, too much of that. But honestly? That's not how I see it. What I see are people who spend their lives faking it, bowing down just to avoid problems, and then complaining that no one respects them. You're always responsible for the way people treat you. Most of the time, people either fear me or handle me with care, and that works just fine for me. Obviously, it doesn't sit well with everyone, and adults usually don't appreciate my independent mindset. That's their problem.

Alright, I have to admit that lately, my temper has been getting me into trouble. No way I'm turning into one of those spineless people I can't stand, but I think I might need to be a little more careful… This past week has been brutal!

After pissing off most of my new teachers and racking up a few disciplinary notes, my parents decided to "tighten the screws" until the end of the year. I'll let you imagine the wonderful atmosphere at home…

Monday morning. My new pair of flats is nowhere to be found.

—— Courtney. Sixteen. A Short Fuse. ——

"Mom, did you move my blue flats?"

"Yes, Courtney, they were lying around in the hallway."

"Ugh, so where are they now?!"

"Hey, watch your tone! Don't start!"

"No, you don't start! Where did you put them?!"

"Courtney, you better change your attitude right now. I believe we had a little talk about this yesterday! Excuse me for trying to keep the house organized!"

"I don't care about that! Where are my shoes?!"

It all went downhill from there. Huge argument. To keep myself from saying something I'd regret, I slammed the door and stormed out, putting on an old pair of sneakers. And bam! That felt good. Only problem? First period was math, and the teacher had warned us he'd randomly pick a few students to hand in their homework. If I get called, I'm screwed. Not because I didn't do it—no, that would be too simple. Because I rushed out of the house so fast that I left my assignment sitting right there on my desk. If he picks me, I'm doomed, and I can already feel my blood boiling. No way I'm taking the blame for something I actually did.

You see where this is going?

Yeah.

— *Courtney. Sixteen. A Short Fuse.* —

"Nooo way! No no no! Not me, sir!"

"Can you explain what's going on, Courtney?"

He's one of those teachers who insists on addressing us formally, like it somehow means he respects us as adults. Yeah, right. If that were true, he'd actually listen to me.

"I did it, sir, I swear!"

"Then hand me your assignment, and we'll move on."

"It's... Still on my desk at home."

"Courtney... I don't have time for these ridiculous excuses. So this is how you're starting the year? Fine."

"I'm telling you, I did it!"

"You're getting an F."

"Are you kidding me?! This is insane!"

"Excuse me?"

"You're completely out of your mind. I did your dumb exercises, I'll bring them tomorrow, and that's that."

"Alright, Courtney. You've got detention."

I knocked over everything on my desk. Everything. Including

— *Courtney. Sixteen. A Short Fuse.* —

Caleb's stuff—my seatmate, a kind of uptight nerd who looked like a startled kitten. Which only made me even angrier. The teacher called for a hall monitor through the window, and just like that, I was being escorted straight to the principal's office. Fantastic. Perfect. Thanks, Mom. All she had to do was tell me where she put my damn shoes. She's gonna pay for this. And the worst part? She'll probably have the nerve to blame me for losing my temper in class.

I can't take it anymore. I feel like I'm about to lose it—for real this time. That's exactly what's running through my head when *Mr. Mustache* asks me what happened. Do I even need to mention that he didn't appreciate my tone of voice?

At lunch, I meet up with Jake, my best friend. The great thing about him is that he gets me. He actually finds my temper kind of funny. But today, he seems off. Head down, pushing his chicken sandwich around his plate, giving me quick, short answers when I ask about his day—just enough to keep me from bringing up mine. Since we're not in the same class, this is my chance to think about something else. And then, out of nowhere, he blurts out:

"You're messing up, Courtney."

"What now? What did I do this time?"

"Everyone at school heard about your math class tantrum."

I can feel it rising instantly. The heat, the anger. I see red. I feel like doing something reckless. And I think it's right at this

— *Courtney. Sixteen. A Short Fuse.* —

moment that I finally realize something isn't right. I'm on the verge of losing it again, ready to snap at the only person who actually gets me. But I hold back.

The rest of the day drags by in a haze of frustration. Every second seems to add to my anger, yet deep down, I know Jake is right. I have to get a grip. But how?

After school, I head straight to the café behind my house, the only place where I can think in peace. His words keep replaying in my head. I have to do something.

Footsteps pull me from my thoughts. Of course, it's Jake. He always knows where to find me. Always shows up when I need him most. He sits down beside me without a word. For a few minutes, we just sit there in silence, watching the kids play on the sidewalk across the street.

"You're letting your anger eat you up from the inside. You deserve better than that."

"I don't know how else to be, Jake. It feels like everyone is against me."

"If you keep fighting everything and everyone, you're going to lose the people who actually care about you. We've been friends for a long time, and it sucks to see you like this."

His words hit me harder than I expected.

Jake usually laughs at my outbursts—he finds them

— *Courtney. Sixteen. A Short Fuse.* —

entertaining. But this time, he's serious. And that seriousness makes me think.

"People piss me off. Situations piss me off…"

Jake shakes his head.

"You should try talking to your parents tonight. Really talking. Not yelling. It might actually change things."

Maybe he's right. Maybe I should try a different approach.

That evening, back home, I find my mom in the kitchen. I take a deep breath and decide to follow Jake's advice.

"Mom, can I talk to you?"

She looks a little surprised by my calm tone but smiles.

"Of course, Courtney. What's on your mind?"

I sit down at the table, trying to gather my thoughts.

"I'm sorry about this morning. I got mad over nothing. It's just… I'm stressed. School, teachers, all of it. And I know I make things hard at home too."

My mom takes my hands in hers.

"I'm going to try to do better. Thanks, Mom."

— *Courtney. Sixteen. A Short Fuse.* —

The next day, I find a note on my desk, written in my homeroom teacher's handwriting:

Courtney, I reread your introduction sheet. I didn't take you seriously enough, and I owe you an apology. I realize that you genuinely want to find meaning in your education, so I went ahead and signed you up for a college and career fair happening over the next two weekends—Saturday and Sunday, from 8 AM to 6 PM. Hopefully, you'll find a program that interests you.

Best,
Mr. Callahan

No, this guy is insane! Two whole weekends ruined?! He's messing with me, for sure. This is payback. No way I'm letting this slide!

Throughout the entire class, I stare him down. Like the Mona Lisa, my eyes follow him from one end of the room to the other. He pretends not to notice. At the end of the lesson, I march up to his desk.

"I'm not interested in the career fair."

"Oh, that's a shame. But it's too little late now—you're already signed up."

"Seriously? You couldn't have asked me first?"

"It seemed like you were looking for some direction…"

— *Courtney. Sixteen. A Short Fuse.* —

"Mr. Callahan, I'm not going."

"It's mandatory, Courtney. You're signed up."

"Why are you even doing this?!"

"Because I have a sense of humor, just like you."

I stare at him blankly.

"It was a joke, Courtney. That fair doesn't exist. I just wanted to show you that you're not the only one who knows how to mess with people."

I leave his classroom and find myself lingering in the hallway, thinking it over.

Yes, he really got me. And yes, it's fair game. But I didn't get angry, and that's not bad. He got me, I have to admit, and maybe it's his way of offering a truce. I'm surprised by these thoughts. Normally, I would have felt humiliated and lost my temper. But not this time. I go back to see him.

"Mr. Callahan, I just wanted to say thank you."

"Oh?"

"You just made me realize something—I need to accept from others what I allow myself."

"Courtney, your anger is a signal. It means there are things

— *Courtney. Sixteen. A Short Fuse.* —

inside you that need attention. If you're open to it, we can work together to figure out what's going on and how you can express your emotions in healthier ways. I've spoken with some of your past teachers—I know you're a great kid. Smart, sharp, and full of potential."

"Thanks, Mr. Callahan..."

And he did help me. Not by trying to erase my anger, but by showing me how to channel it differently.

"A lot of things in this world deserve our intolerance," Mr. Callahan said. "You carry a fire inside you, and that's a good thing. But you need to direct it toward what's truly unacceptable."

"Like what?"

"Injustice. Poverty, for example."

"I don't get it..."

"Get involved! Put your energy into something that actually matters."

I had never thought about it that way. And yet, it was so obvious.

My anger—this raw, untamed force—could be channeled into something constructive. I could use it to be part of something bigger than myself. Jake was right. Mr. Callahan

― *Courtney. Sixteen. A Short Fuse.* ―

was right. Even my parents were right. I deserved more than to let my rage eat me alive. And for the first time, I believed I could actually make a difference.

That night, Jake met me at our usual spot, the little café behind my house. I told him everything—about Callahan, about what I'd realized, about how I was planning to join an activist group Callahan had mentioned.

He looked at me with a knowing smile.

"You know, Courtney, you've always been amazing. But now? Now you're becoming extraordinary."

His words hit me hard. For the first time, I felt at peace—with myself, and with the world around me.

The Bully

— *The Bully* —

All these anti-bullying posters at school are so annoying. Seriously, it's just for weaklings. Nowadays, you crack one little joke, and suddenly you're getting called in.

My older brother told me about his high school years, and let me tell you, it was a whole different world. Especially since he was in a sports academy program, and the hazing was brutal. Even I think some of it was messed up. Like the time all the new recruits had to march naked across the schoolyard while getting pelted with open yogurt cups. Or the time they had to run laps in the scorching midday sun while getting whipped with judo belts the entire time.

"No one complained, it was just tradition," he said. "You had to take it without flinching. It was a way to prove you were tough. And besides, every rookie knew that one day, they'd get their turn to welcome the new guys."

"That was still pretty violent, though."

"Yeah, well… Life is violent! It was part of toughening up."

Honestly, even if things were rough back then, I'd still take that era over mine. I don't get how someone can call themselves a victim of bullying without feeling ashamed. Just don't let it happen! You can spot a victim from a mile away… They carry it with them.

I've already been called in twice. Once by my homeroom teacher, once by the dean. "Connor, this is unacceptable." "Connor, do you realize what you're doing?" What are you

— *The Bully* —

even supposed to say to that? When a girl from our class posts pictures of herself, she knows people are going to see them, right? What part of "social media" doesn't she get? She wants comments? Well, I comment.

Okay, maybe I go a little hard sometimes, but that's part of the game. You can't expect only "*Omg, you're so gorgeous, babe.*"

Same with Nathan, that clueless nerd. I don't care if he's a brainiac. He likes math, French, history—good for him. He also likes having the best grades? Fine by me. Me, I like PE, and that's where I want to be the best. So in basketball or soccer, I figure I can shove him around or tackle him as much as needed. That's just sports. You'd have to be crazy to call that bullying! And yet, he starts whining, and that drives me nuts. Yeah, I mess with him a little, but that's part of the game. If he can't handle it, he should just get a doctor's note and sit out.

Anyway, I always thought bullying was just some modern-day nonsense. A trend.

Or rather, I used to think that… The person talking to you now has changed a lot since then.

Let's just say I had a little mishap that made me change my perspective. It all started with Brandon' arrival…

It's the end of the second semester. Nothing out of the ordinary. Then one day, I notice a new face at the back of the

— *The Bully* —

classroom. Brandon. He looked like a decent kid, nothing intimidating about him. I wouldn't have even paid attention to him if he hadn't quickly become friends with Nathan. A strange duo, to be honest. Brandon had already repeated two grades and couldn't afford to fail his junior year. So, he quickly figured out who could help him a little. What I didn't immediately realize, though, was that they had formed some kind of unspoken pact, a deal where each of them benefited from the other's strengths.

And what exactly were Brandon's strengths? You'll find out soon enough…

Beneath his quiet, almost friendly demeanor, Brandon was tough, really tough. The kind of guy who's all the more intimidating because he never loses his cool. The kind of calm before a storm that hasn't arrived yet, but when it does, you just know it's going to hit hard. Brandon had made it his mission to protect Nathan. More than that, he was his guardian angel. But not just any guardian angel—an overzealous one, always a step ahead, scanning for anything that could be a threat to his new ally. And you've probably guessed it by now… I was the target. Even though I hadn't had a single run-in with Nathan in a while, he still feared me. And Brandon? He could sense it.

Everything spiraled out of control one morning between classes. Out of nowhere, Brandon slammed into me—hard. A brutal shoulder check to the back, as if I wasn't walking fast enough. But like always, the hallway was packed. The impact was so strong that I went straight to the ground. Ready to

The Bully

fight, I got up, only to find myself staring into his eyes, and what I saw there froze me in place. A kind of hatred I couldn't even describe. One more move, and he would have torn me apart right there, in front of everyone. What else could I do but walk away like nothing had happened?

It was humiliating. A full-on public humiliation, and a lot of people saw it. The whole afternoon, it was all anyone talked about.

I brought it up with my friends a few days later, but the conversation was awkward. No one really knew what to say. The attack had been completely unprovoked. I thought about getting back at him, but let's be real—the idea of facing off against that guy didn't exactly thrill me. Better to let time do its thing. Soon enough, everyone would forget.

Turns out, Brandon had no intention of leaving me alone. In class, I could feel his eyes on me constantly. Whenever I answered a question, he'd let out a quiet chuckle—just soft enough to stay under the teachers' radar but loud enough to get under my skin. On my way home, I'd catch glimpses of him behind me, always just far enough away to make it seem coincidental. On social media, he liked every single one of my posts without ever commenting, like some kind of silent reminder that he was still there. Before long, I found myself caught in a strange question: was he obsessed with me, or was I the one becoming obsessed with him?

The worst part was probably not being able to talk about it. After spending so much time criticizing my classmates for

The Bully

being "too fragile," I couldn't afford to show the slightest sign of weakness in front of everyone. As for bringing it up with the school staff—out of the question. Getting labeled a snitch by someone like Brandon would be the worst possible move. And yet, what had started as a simple shove in a crowded hallway quickly escalated into a full-blown campaign of terror, carefully orchestrated by Brandon.

The day after our first altercation, Brandon wasted no time in stepping up his harassment. As soon as I walked into class, I could feel his piercing gaze on me. Every move I made, he was there—like a looming shadow. At first, I tried to ignore him, hoping he'd get bored and move on. But he didn't. If anything, he seemed to enjoy it even more, taking a twisted pleasure in making my life hell.

The worst was yet to come, with his actions growing more insidious by the day. I think he wanted to drive me crazy. My locker became his favorite target. Every day, I'd find insulting notes slipped inside—scribbled on torn pieces of paper. "Coward," "Pathetic," "Loser", the same words, over and over. One day, I found something even worse. A photo of me, taken without my knowledge, with the word "Victim" scrawled across my forehead in red ink. It sent a chill down my spine. How was he taking these pictures without me noticing? Was he always there, lurking in the shadows, watching me?

At home, things weren't any better. My parents had no idea what was going on. I couldn't bring myself to tell them. How was I supposed to explain that I—Connor—the tough guy,

— The Bully —

the one who mocked weakness in others, was now a victim of bullying? Yes. *Bullying*. That was the word. I was too ashamed to admit it. All I could do was bottle up the anxiety.

The walk home from school, usually uneventful, had turned into a nightmare. Every shadow, every noise made me jump. I knew he was out there somewhere, waiting, watching. At night, I barely slept, haunted by the thought that he could show up at any moment. In my dreams, Brandon was always chasing me, his eyes gleaming with malice.

That left my older brother. I felt embarrassed bringing it up to him, but what else could I do? I was losing my grip.

"You ever had someone try to mess with your head?"

"Go on."

"I don't know… It's nothing specific. He's just on my case all the time."

"You guys fought yet?"

"Not yet."

"Then what are you waiting for? If you don't put him in his place now, he'll walk all over you. At the very least, you need to put some pressure on him."

"The thing is… he's weird."

―― *The Bully* ――

"Weird how?"

"I feel like this could get really bad…"

"Wait, what did you do to him?"

"Uh… nothing… that's the thing."

"You're telling me you're getting bullied?"

"No, it's not like that, but…"

"But what?"

"I don't know, it's weird. He's always pushing me, testing me for no reason. I think he's mainly trying to stand up for some guy I messed with a little at the start of the year."

"So let me get this straight… You're getting bullied, Connor."

My brother had figured it out. There was no point in trying to hide the truth. I broke down, crying like a little kid, and to my surprise, he didn't mock me. Quite the opposite. He put his hands on my shoulders, made me lift my head, and spoke in a calm, almost wise tone I had never heard from him before.

"You're not going to let this slide, Connor. But you're also not going to make things worse. In situations like this, there are only two options. Either you talk to a teacher about it, or you confront him yourself."

— *The Bully* —

Three days later, an unexpected announcement reached our ears: a guest speaker was coming to talk to students about bullying. The news spread quickly around the school, triggering mixed reactions. Most students laughed it off— exactly as I would have a few weeks ago. As for me, I was struggling to hide my nerves.

The day arrived, and all the students were gathered in the large auditorium. The speaker, a woman in her forties with a kind gaze and a reassuring smile, introduced herself as Ms. Caldwell. She began by explaining what bullying was, its consequences, and most importantly, the need to break the silence. Her words hit me hard. Every sentence felt like it was aimed directly at me...

After a rather somber introduction, during which she shared the story of her own daughter's bullying, Ms. Caldwell opened the floor for discussion. She encouraged students to share their experiences, ask questions, or simply express their thoughts on the subject. A heavy silence settled over the room. No one dared to speak. I could feel my heart pounding harder and harder. My palms were sweaty, and an internal battle raged within me.

Then, almost without realizing it, my hand went up. I could feel all eyes turning toward me, including Brandon's. A wave of courage surged through me, and I stood up. My voice was slightly unsteady as I took a deep breath before speaking.

"Hi, my name is Connor. I want to share something. For a long time, I thought bullying was just a thing for weak people.

— *The Bully* —

I took part in mocking others, in criticizing... But recently, I learned what it feels like to be a target."

A murmur spread through the room. Brandon stared at me intently, his expression unreadable.

"There's a student here—Brandon—who has been harassing me for weeks. He humiliates me, follows me, terrorizes me. And I didn't know what to do. I was afraid of looking like a snitch, afraid to admit that I couldn't handle it on my own."

Now, all eyes turned to Brandon, whose face showed a flicker of both frustration and disbelief. Ms. Caldwell remained silent, letting me continue.

"Today, I want to say stop. Brandon, I'm asking you to call a truce. I'm asking you to leave me alone. I get it, you wanted to stand up for your friend. And I hate that it took going through this myself to understand what I put him through."

Total silence. Everyone was hanging on my every word. Brandon, however, seemed caught off guard. For a few moments, he didn't move. Then, he stood up and walked toward me, his eyes locked onto mine. A shiver ran down my spine, but I stayed put, determined not to back down. *If he hits me in front of everyone*, I thought, *we're both done for*. He'll get expelled, but I'll take the humiliation of a lifetime.

In a low voice, he replied:

"I wasn't expecting this. Connor, I'm sorry. It wasn't fair. I... I

— *The Bully* —

thought I was teaching you a lesson, but it went too far."

A wave of relief swept through the room. Brandon and I stood there, looking at each other, both aware of the weight of the moment. Then, Ms. Caldwell spoke, her voice gentle yet firm:

"What we just witnessed is an example of real courage. Admitting your mistakes, apologizing, and choosing to change, that is true strength. Thank you, Connor. Thank you, Brandon. This was a powerful moment for all of us."

Brandon and I never really became friends, but I did grow closer to Nathan. Turns out he's actually a great guy. Behind his bookish persona, he has a sharp sense of humor. Sometimes, we spend entire breaks trying to imitate each other, cracking up in laughter.

But the real difference is something else entirely. Now I understand the value of humor, and the difference between laughing at someone and laughing with them.

And that makes all the difference.

A Filter Between You and Yourself

— A Filter Between You and Yourself —

At first glance, she's a typical teenager. She drags her feet. She sulks. She's bored about half the time. She's proud. She's full of ambition... Without making the slightest effort to achieve anything!

Well, not quite like the others. Rose is almost a caricature of a high school sophomore. She has the charm—her humor, her generosity, that mischievous spark that makes her so likable—but she also takes teenage flaws to a whole new level. The worst part? Her relationship with screens, especially her phone.

Every morning, as soon as she wakes up, Rose grabs her phone with a steady hand, even though her eyes are still stuck shut with sleep. She squints, rubs them, trying to reconnect with a brain that isn't quite awake yet. The priority? Checking the notifications that piled up overnight. Right away! Why? And why not? That's how she starts her day: scrolling through social media, replying to messages, checking out the latest trending videos, hoping to get noticed for her comments. A teenage life, but taken to the extreme, as you'll soon see.

This morning ritual often made her miss family breakfast, which particularly irritated her mother.

"Rose, put your phone down and come eat! You do this every morning, it's unbearable!"

Her response was always the same:

A Filter Between You and Yourself

"Just a sec, Mom, I'm finishing something…"

Of course, she never actually finished that "something." Because, really, it wasn't meant to be finished. One post was always followed by another, and another, and when the next one was dull, there was no doubt the one after that would be worth her attention. A kind of compulsion, an obsession.

For Rose, the digital world was like real life, but faster, denser. It made her feel more alive, fueled her imagination and desires. Compared to it, everyday life felt painfully dull.

Things weren't any better at school. Rose had mastered the art of hiding her phone under the desk during class. She got bored easily and found chatting online with her virtual friends far more interesting than whatever was being taught. But despite her skill, she occasionally got caught in the act—a habit that was starting to get her into trouble with her teachers.

"Rose, I assume you're busy researching quadratic equations in their canonical form, am I right?"

What could she say to her math teacher?

"Uh… Yeah… Well, no, not exactly. Sorry, sir…"

It's surprising she managed to keep hold of her precious phone for so long, but as it turns out, Rose was actually a good student, a very good one. She got away with almost everything because her grades were excellent. "She seems distracted, but she's paying attention," her English teacher had said during the class review meeting. In short, she'd get caught, mumble an apology, pretend to focus—while already thinking about what she'd comment or post later.

Sometimes, being naturally gifted at school is a kind of curse. For most people, you have to hit rock bottom before kicking hard enough to push yourself back up. Failure can be a good thing—it's a wake-up call. But for Rose, always floating effortlessly at the surface, nothing ever seemed to set off the alarm.

Her friends, however, were starting to get annoyed. During breaks, Rose remained glued to her screen, ignoring the conversations and bursts of laughter around her. When someone tried to get her attention, she would respond with nothing more than a sound or a grunt.

"Rose, you're overdoing it. You're always on your phone. Just say it if we're bothering you!"

"It's not that you're bothering me, I'm just busy, that's all."

Did she realize how harsh that sounded? Apparently not. In reality, Rose was losing touch with the world around her. In her world, everything moved at the speed of a scroll. Everything was lights, colors, aesthetics, promises. She didn't even particularly dream of becoming an influencer—she simply wanted to stay connected to the frantic buzz of social media.

― *A Filter Between You and Yourself* ―

For her, it could easily be called a drug.

So much so that when her mother asked about the topic of her Moral and Civic Education presentation and got no answer, she threw at her:

"You're really starting to annoy us, Rose. Do your presentation on your phone—at least that way, you'll be sure not to part with it!"

But... Wasn't that actually an excellent topic?! Rose didn't reply but started mulling over the idea. After all, it was a real social issue, and this would finally give her a chance to respond to all those busybodies. Perfect. She got to work.

For the first time, Rose took a real break from her frantic activity on social media to dive into deeper research. The topic was broad, somewhat complex, but most importantly, it directly concerned her. She wanted to understand, analyze, and prove that she wasn't obsessed, that there was something constructive in her behavior. Everyone has their own way of seeing and experiencing the world, after all! Some people read the newspaper, some watch TV (her parents weren't exactly role models in that regard...), some spend hours buried in books, and others choose to create a social life online. In the end, those are all just different ways of staying in the virtual world. At least, that was the argument she initially planned to defend...

As she dug deeper into her research, Rose discovered the history of communication technologies, the evolution of

— A Filter Between You and Yourself —

social networks, and the numerous studies on their psychological impact. She was surprised by the extent of the reported negative effects—anxiety, depression, sleep disorders, low self-esteem. She also looked for the benefits—access to information, maintaining long-distance relationships, professional opportunities. It was like uncovering both sides of the same coin. There was even an old Greek concept for it: pharmakon. Something that is both a poison and a remedy. She liked the idea. It felt clearer, easier to defend than her original argument. That would be her thesis!

But her presentation gradually took on a different shape. She decided to structure it around three main points: the history of social media, its effects on society, and finally, a personal reflection on her own usage. She made sure to include testimonials, statistics, and even examples from her own experience.

When the day of the presentation arrived, Rose was ready. Standing in front of the class, she began with a direct question:

"Who here checks their phone first thing in the morning?"

A few hands hesitantly went up. Rose smiled, feeling more confident.

"Me too. And that's where my presentation begins."

She spoke with passion, sharing her discoveries, her

— *A Filter Between You and Yourself* —

concerns, but also the positive aspects she had found. Her classmates, initially skeptical, grew more attentive as she went on. The history teacher, who also handled the civic education class, watched her with an impressed look. It was rare for students to show such sincerity.

To conclude, she shared a personal reflection:

"Using social media isn't a problem in itself. It's how we use it, and the importance we give it, that can become one. Maybe it's time to find some balance. I should know, believe me…"

That day, Rose had managed to captivate her audience. Even better—through her research, she had managed to captivate herself. For the first time in a long while, she felt a genuine sense of pride—not for the number of likes or comments, but for something more tangible, more real.

And then came Jean's question:

"And what about now? Are you going to throw your phone away?"

Okay, that wasn't exactly pleasant, but fair enough… Hard to answer. She mumbled something unconvincing about taking the time to think it through and how awareness was already a big step forward.

When she got home, she made a decision. Her phone would stay off for at least an hour each morning… Enough time to

— A Filter Between You and Yourself —

enjoy a real breakfast with her family. It wouldn't be easy, but she wanted to try. For herself, for her loved ones, and because deep down, she knew the real world was worth a little effort.

The first morning, her hand shot out from under the covers on autopilot, ready to switch off airplane mode and hear, like every day, the familiar chime of notifications. But she caught herself—startled by how deeply ingrained the habit was. The same thing happened the next day. But gradually, the resolution took hold.

And so, the cycle began to break. Little by little, Rose learned to rediscover life without filters, without the endless scrolling. She learned to appreciate simple moments, to reconnect with her friends, and above all, with herself. The transition was not without difficulties, but she understood that every small step was worth it. She didn't completely give up her digital world, but she learned to master it, to integrate it into her daily life in a more balanced way.

In the end, the real screen between oneself and oneself wasn't the phone, but the habits we don't dare to question. Rose had chosen to break through it, and that decision marked the beginning of a new adventure—one that was far richer and more fulfilling.

Is this the end of the story?

No. Absolutely not...

— *A Filter Between You and Yourself* —

In real life, nothing is ever simple, especially when it comes to breaking a bad habit. They say the brain needs twenty-one days to form a new behavior. And twenty-one days? That's a long time. Very long!

After two weeks of her new morning routine, one notification in particular caught Rose's attention. An old virtual friend, a rising influencer, had invited her to take part in a challenge that promised to go viral. How could she resist the lure of digital fame, even if it was only hypothetical?

Rose hesitated, torn between her recent resolutions and the temptation to dive back into the frenzy of social media, into that thrilling world. She gave in. She spent hours perfecting her short videos, recording them in secret, and engaging with her followers. The unfortunate part? The likes and comments flooded in. Rose felt more alive than ever, yet paradoxically, she also sensed the return of an inner emptiness.

For the first time, her grades dropped. Her worried parents tried to talk to her, but she shut down, retreating even further into the digital world to escape her real-life problems.

One evening, as she felt particularly alone despite the dozens of notifications, her presentation came back to mind. She realized she had to make a choice. A definitive choice. She had a moment of recklessness—one that was also a stroke of genius. In any case, it was a remarkable act of courage.

The first few days were tough. She felt lost, disconnected from the world—especially since her friends seemed to be

― *A Filter Between You and Yourself* ―

avoiding her after her relapse. Little by little, she began to rediscover simple pleasures: reading, chatting with her parents, and taking walks at dusk.

One evening, as she returned from a walk—sad but determined to keep her promise to herself—she heard a soft meow. At her feet sat a tiny white kitten, staring at her with an intense gaze that seemed to say, Take me with you. She bent down, picked it up in her hands, stroked its fur, and suddenly burst into tears. There was joy in adopting this little creature—she knew her parents would agree—but there was also a terrifying thought: if she had been on her phone, she never would have noticed the abandoned ball of fur. What would have happened to it then?

The real world, far less dazzling than the digital one, was infinitely richer and more rewarding.

On her birthday, her parents gave her a camera. Not a smartphone, but an actual camera! They wanted to show her that she could capture and share the beauty of the world she had rediscovered. Rose teared up again, deeply moved by their gesture. She discovered a new passion. Photographing her surroundings meant exploring different angles, compositions, and perspectives.

In the end, Rose hadn't just broken free from her dependence on screens. She had learned to create her own balance between reality and imagination.

The most meaningful connection is the one we have with

ourselves and those around us. No screen will ever be able to replace that.

Tell us what you thought of this book by scanning the QR code—we read all your reviews!

Amazon.com

Amazon.co.uk

Made in the USA
Coppell, TX
08 June 2025